HINDI

VOCABULARY

ENGLISH-HINDI

The most useful words
To expand your lexicon and sharpen
your language skills

3000 words

Hindi vocabulary for English speakers - 3000 words

By Andrey Taranov

T&P Books vocabularies are intended for helping you learn, memorize and review foreign words. The dictionary is divided into themes, covering all major spheres of everyday activities, business, science, culture, etc.

The process of learning words using T&P Books' theme-based dictionaries gives you the following advantages:

- Correctly grouped source information predetermines success at subsequent stages of word memorization
- Availability of words derived from the same root allowing memorization of word units (rather than separate words)
- Small units of words facilitate the process of establishing associative links needed for consolidation of vocabulary
- Level of language knowledge can be estimated by the number of learned words

T&P Books Publishing
www.tpbooks.com

ISBN: 978-1-78616-610-4

This book is also available in E-book formats.
Please visit www.tpbooks.com or the major online bookstores.

HINDI VOCABULARY
for English speakers

T&P Books vocabularies are intended to help you learn, memorize, and review foreign words. The vocabulary contains over 3000 commonly used words arranged thematically.

- Vocabulary contains the most commonly used words
- Recommended as an addition to any language course
- Meets the needs of beginners and advanced learners of foreign languages
- Convenient for daily use, revision sessions, and self-testing activities
- Allows you to assess your vocabulary

Special features of the vocabulary

- Words are organized according to their meaning, not alphabetically
- Words are presented in three columns to facilitate the reviewing and self-testing processes
- Words in groups are divided into small blocks to facilitate the learning process
- The vocabulary offers a convenient and simple transcription of each foreign word

The vocabulary has 101 topics including:

Basic Concepts, Numbers, Colors, Months, Seasons, Units of Measurement, Clothing & Accessories, Food & Nutrition, Restaurant, Family Members, Relatives, Character, Feelings, Emotions, Diseases, City, Town, Sightseeing, Shopping, Money, House, Home, Office, Working in the Office, Import & Export, Marketing, Job Search, Sports, Education, Computer, Internet, Tools, Nature, Countries, Nationalities and more ...

T&P BOOKS' THEME-BASED DICTIONARIES

The Correct System for Memorizing Foreign Words

Acquiring vocabulary is one of the most important elements of learning a foreign language, because words allow us to express our thoughts, ask questions, and provide answers. An inadequate vocabulary can impede communication with a foreigner and make it difficult to understand a book or movie well.

The pace of activity in all spheres of modern life, including the learning of modern languages, has increased. Today, we need to memorize large amounts of information (grammar rules, foreign words, etc.) within a short period. However, this does not need to be difficult. All you need to do is to choose the right training materials, learn a few special techniques, and develop your individual training system.

Having a system is critical to the process of language learning. Many people fail to succeed in this regard; they cannot master a foreign language because they fail to follow a system comprised of selecting materials, organizing lessons, arranging new words to be learned, and so on. The lack of a system causes confusion and eventually, lowers self-confidence.

T&P Books' theme-based dictionaries can be included in the list of elements needed for creating an effective system for learning foreign words. These dictionaries were specially developed for learning purposes and are meant to help students effectively memorize words and expand their vocabulary.

Generally speaking, the process of learning words consists of three main elements:

- Reception (creation or acquisition) of a training material, such as a word list
- Work aimed at memorizing new words
- Work aimed at reviewing the learned words, such as self-testing

All three elements are equally important since they determine the quality of work and the final result. All three processes require certain skills and a well-thought-out approach.

New words are often encountered quite randomly when learning a foreign language and it may be difficult to include them all in a unified list. As a result, these words remain written on scraps of paper, in book margins, textbooks, and so on. In order to systematize such words, we have to create and continually update a "book of new words." A paper notebook, a netbook, or a tablet PC can be used for these purposes.

This "book of new words" will be your personal, unique list of words. However, it will only contain the words that you came across during the learning process. For example, you might have written down the words "Sunday," "Tuesday," and "Friday." However, there are additional words for days of the week, for example, "Saturday," that are missing, and your list of words would be incomplete. Using a theme dictionary, in addition to the "book of new words," is a reasonable solution to this problem.

The theme-based dictionary may serve as the basis for expanding your vocabulary.

It will be your big "book of new words" containing the most frequently used words of a foreign language already included. There are quite a few theme-based dictionaries available, and you should ensure that you make the right choice in order to get the maximum benefit from your purchase.

Therefore, we suggest using theme-based dictionaries from T&P Books Publishing as an aid to learning foreign words. Our books are specially developed for effective use in the sphere of vocabulary systematization, expansion and review.

Theme-based dictionaries are not a magical solution to learning new words. However, they can serve as your main database to aid foreign-language acquisition. Apart from theme dictionaries, you can have copybooks for writing down new words, flash cards, glossaries for various texts, as well as other resources; however, a good theme dictionary will always remain your primary collection of words.

T&P Books' theme-based dictionaries are specialty books that contain the most frequently used words in a language.

The main characteristic of such dictionaries is the division of words into themes. For example, the *City* theme contains the words "street," "crossroads," "square," "fountain," and so on. The *Talking* theme might contain words like "to talk," "to ask," "question," and "answer".

All the words in a theme are divided into smaller units, each comprising 3–5 words. Such an arrangement improves the perception of words and makes the learning process less tiresome. Each unit contains a selection of words with similar meanings or identical roots. This allows you to learn words in small groups and establish other associative links that have a positive effect on memorization.

The words on each page are placed in three columns: a word in your native language, its translation, and its transcription. Such positioning allows for the use of techniques for effective memorization. After closing the translation column, you can flip through and review foreign words, and vice versa. "This is an easy and convenient method of review – one that we recommend you do often."

Our theme-based dictionaries contain transcriptions for all the foreign words. Unfortunately, none of the existing transcriptions are able to convey the exact nuances of foreign pronunciation. That is why we recommend using the transcriptions only as a supplementary learning aid. Correct pronunciation can only be acquired with the help of sound. Therefore our collection includes audio theme-based dictionaries.

The process of learning words using T&P Books' theme-based dictionaries gives you the following advantages:

- You have correctly grouped source information, which predetermines your success at subsequent stages of word memorization
- Availability of words derived from the same root (lazy, lazily, lazybones), allowing you to memorize word units instead of separate words
- Small units of words facilitate the process of establishing associative links needed for consolidation of vocabulary
- You can estimate the number of learned words and hence your level of language knowledge
- The dictionary allows for the creation of an effective and high-quality revision process
- You can revise certain themes several times, modifying the revision methods and techniques
- Audio versions of the dictionaries help you to work out the pronunciation of words and develop your skills of auditory word perception

The T&P Books' theme-based dictionaries are offered in several variants differing in the number of words: 1.500, 3.000, 5.000, 7.000, and 9.000 words. There are also dictionaries containing 15,000 words for some language combinations. Your choice of dictionary will depend on your knowledge level and goals.

We sincerely believe that our dictionaries will become your trusty assistant in learning foreign languages and will allow you to easily acquire the necessary vocabulary.

TABLE OF CONTENTS

PRONUNCIATION GUIDE

Letter	Hindi example	T&P phonetic alphabet	English example

Vowels

अ	अक्सर	[a]; [ɑ], [ə]	park; teacher
आ	आगमन	[a:]	calf, palm
इ	इनाम	[i]	shorter than in feet
ई	ईश्वर	[i], [i:]	feet, Peter
उ	उठना	[ʊ]	good, booklet
ऊ	ऊपर	[u:]	pool, room
ऋ	ऋग्वेद	[r, rʲ]	green
ए	एकता	[e:]	longer than in bell
ऐ	ऐनक	[aj]	time, white
ओ	ओला	[o:]	fall, bomb
औ	औरत	[au]	loud, powder
अं	अंजीर	[ŋ]	English, ring
अः	अ से अः	[h]	home, have
ऑ	ऑफिस	[ɒ]	cotton, pocket

Consonants

क	कमरा	[k]	clock, kiss
ख	खिड़की	[kh]	work hard
ग	गरज	[g]	game, gold
घ	घर	[gh]	g aspirated
ङ	डाकू	[ŋ]	English, ring
च	चक्कर	[tʃ]	church, French
छ	छात्र	[tʃh]	hitchhiker
ज	जाना	[dʒ]	joke, general
झ	झलक	[dʒ]	joke, general
ञ	विज्ञान	[n]	canyon, new
ट	मटर	[t]	tourist, trip
ठ	ठेका	[th]	don't have
ड	डंडा	[d]	day, doctor
ढ	ढलान	[d]	day, doctor
ण	क्षण	[n]	retroflex nasal
त	ताकत	[t]	tourist, trip

Letter	Hindi example	T&P phonetic alphabet	English example
थ	थकना	[th]	don't have
द	दरवाज़ा	[d]	day, doctor
ध	धोना	[d]	day, doctor
न	नाई	[n]	sang, thing
प	पिता	[p]	pencil, private
फ	फल	[f]	face, food
ब	बच्चा	[b]	baby, book
भ	भाई	[b]	baby, book
म	माता	[m]	magic, milk
य	याद	[j]	yes, New York
र	रीछ	[r]	rice, radio
ल	लाल	[l]	lace, people
व	वचन	[v]	very, river
श	शिक्षक	[ʃ]	machine, shark
ष	भाषा	[ʃ]	machine, shark
स	सोना	[s]	city, boss
ह	हज़ार	[h]	home, have

Additional consonants

क़	क़लम	[q]	king, club
ख़	ख़बर	[h]	huge, hat
ड़	लड़का	[r]	rice, radio
ढ़	पढ़ना	[r]	rice, radio
ग़	ग़लती	[ɣ]	between [g] and [h]
ज़	ज़िन्दगी	[z]	zebra, please
झ़	ट्रेझ़र	[ʒ]	forge, pleasure
फ़	फ़ौज	[f]	face, food

ABBREVIATIONS
used in the vocabulary

English abbreviations

ab.	-	about
adj	-	adjective
adv	-	adverb
anim.	-	animate
as adj	-	attributive noun used as adjective
e.g.	-	for example
etc.	-	et cetera
fam.	-	familiar
fem.	-	feminine
form.	-	formal
inanim.	-	inanimate
masc.	-	masculine
math	-	mathematics
mil.	-	military
n	-	noun
pl	-	plural
pron.	-	pronoun
sb	-	somebody
sing.	-	singular
sth	-	something
v aux	-	auxiliary verb
vi	-	intransitive verb
vi, vt	-	intransitive, transitive verb
vt	-	transitive verb

Hindi abbreviations

f	-	feminine noun
f pl	-	feminine plural
m	-	masculine noun
m pl	-	masculine plural

BASIC CONCEPTS

1. Pronouns

I, me	मैं	main
you	तुम	tum
he, she, it	वह	vah

we	हम	ham
you (to a group)	आप	āp
they	वे	ve

2. Greetings. Salutations

Hello! (fam.)	नमस्कार!	namaskār!
Hello! (form.)	नमस्ते!	namaste!
Good morning!	नमस्ते!	namaste!
Good afternoon!	नमस्ते!	namaste!
Good evening!	नमस्ते!	namaste!

to say hello	नमस्कार कहना	namaskār kahana
Hi! (hello)	नमस्कार!	namaskār!
greeting (n)	अभिवादन (m)	abhivādan
to greet (vt)	अभिवादन करना	abhivādan karana
How are you?	आप कैसे हैं?	āp kaise hain?
What's new?	क्या हाल है?	kya hāl hai?

Bye-Bye! Goodbye!	अलविदा!	alavida!
See you soon!	फिर मिलेंगे!	fir milenge!
Farewell! (to a friend)	अलिवदा!	alivada!
Farewell! (form.)	अलविदा!	alavida!
to say goodbye	अलविदा कहना	alavida kahana
So long!	अलविदा!	alavida!

Thank you!	धन्यवाद!	dhanyavād!
Thank you very much!	बहुत बहुत शुक्रिया!	bahut bahut shukriya!
You're welcome	कोई बात नहीं	koī bāt nahin
Don't mention it!	कोई बात नहीं	koī bāt nahin
It was nothing	कोई बात नहीं	koī bāt nahin

Excuse me! (fam.)	माफ़ कीजिएगा!	māf kījiega!
Excuse me! (form.)	माफ़ी कीजियेगा!	māfī kījiega!
to excuse (forgive)	माफ़ करना	māf karana
to apologize (vi)	माफ़ी मांगना	māfī māngana

My apologies	मुझे माफ़ कीजिएगा	mujhe māf kījiega
I'm sorry!	मुझे माफ़ कीजिएगा।	mujhe māf kījiega!
to forgive (vt)	माफ़ करना	māf karana
please (adv)	कृप्या	krpya

Don't forget!	भूलना नहीं!	bhūlana nahin!
Certainly!	ज़रूर!	zarūr!
Of course not!	बिल्कुल नहीं!	bilkul nahin!
Okay! (I agree)	ठीक है!	thīk hai!
That's enough!	बहुत हुआ!	bahut hua!

3. Questions

Who?	कौन?	kaun?
What?	क्या?	kya?
Where? (at, in)	कहाँ?	kahān?
Where (to)?	किधर?	kidhar?
From where?	कहाँ से?	kahān se?
When?	कब?	kab?
Why? (What for?)	क्यों?	kyon?
Why? (~ are you crying?)	क्यों?	kyon?

What for?	किस लिये?	kis liye?
How? (in what way)	कैसे?	kaise?
What? (What kind of ...?)	कौन-सा?	kaun-sa?
Which?	कौन-सा?	kaun-sa?

To whom?	किसको?	kisako?
About whom?	किसके बारे में?	kisake bāre men?
About what?	किसके बारे में?	kisake bāre men?
With whom?	किसके?	kisake?

How many? How much?	कितना?	kitana?
Whose?	किसका?	kisaka?

4. Prepositions

with (accompanied by)	के साथ	ke sāth
without	के बिना	ke bina
to (indicating direction)	की तरफ़	kī taraf
about (talking ~ ...)	के बारे में	ke bāre men
before (in time)	के पहले	ke pahale
in front of ...	के सामने	ke sāmane

under (beneath, below)	के नीचे	ke nīche
above (over)	के ऊपर	ke ūpar
on (atop)	पर	par
from (off, out of)	से	se

of (made from)	से	se
in (e.g., ~ ten minutes)	में	men
over (across the top of)	के ऊपर चढ़कर	ke ūpar charhakar

5. Function words. Adverbs. Part 1

Where? (at, in)	कहाँ?	kahān?
here (adv)	यहाँ	yahān
there (adv)	वहां	vahān

| somewhere (to be) | कहीं | kahīn |
| nowhere (not anywhere) | कहीं नहीं | kahīn nahin |

| by (near, beside) | के पास | ke pās |
| by the window | खिड़की के पास | khirakī ke pās |

Where (to)?	किधर?	kidhar?
here (e.g., come ~!)	इधर	idhar
there (e.g., to go ~)	उधर	udhar
from here (adv)	यहां से	yahān se
from there (adv)	वहां से	vahān se

| close (adv) | पास | pās |
| far (adv) | दूर | dūr |

near (e.g., ~ Paris)	निकट	nikat
nearby (adv)	पास	pās
not far (adv)	दूर नहीं	dūr nahin

left (adj)	बायाँ	bāyān
on the left	बायीं तरफ़	bāyīn taraf
to the left	बायीं तरफ़	bāyīn taraf

right (adj)	दायां	dāyān
on the right	दायीं तरफ़	dāyīn taraf
to the right	दायीं तरफ़	dāyīn taraf

in front (adv)	सामने	sāmane
front (as adj)	सामने का	sāmane ka
ahead (the kids ran ~)	आगे	āge

behind (adv)	पीछे	pīchhe
from behind	पीछे से	pīchhe se
back (towards the rear)	पीछे	pīchhe

| middle | बीच (m) | bīch |
| in the middle | बीच में | bīch men |

| at the side | कोने में | kone men |
| everywhere (adv) | सभी | sabhī |

around (in all directions)	आस-पास	ās-pās
from inside	अंदर से	andar se
somewhere (to go)	कहीं	kahīn
straight (directly)	सीधे	sīdhe
back (e.g., come ~)	वापस	vāpas
from anywhere	कहीं से भी	kahīn se bhī
from somewhere	कहीं से	kahīn se
firstly (adv)	पहले	pahale
secondly (adv)	दूसरा	dūsara
thirdly (adv)	तीसरा	tīsara
suddenly (adv)	अचानक	achānak
at first (in the beginning)	शुरू में	shurū men
for the first time	पहली बार	pahalī bār
long before ...	बहुत समय पहले ...	bahut samay pahale ...
anew (over again)	नई शुरुआत	naī shurūāt
for good (adv)	हमेशा के लिए	hamesha ke lie
never (adv)	कभी नहीं	kabhī nahin
again (adv)	फिर से	fir se
now (adv)	अब	ab
often (adv)	अकसर	akasar
then (adv)	तब	tab
urgently (quickly)	तत्काल	tatkāl
usually (adv)	आमतौर पर	āmataur par
by the way, ...	प्रसंगवश	prasangavash
possible (that is ~)	मुमकिन	mumakin
probably (adv)	संभव	sambhav
maybe (adv)	शायद	shāyad
besides ...	इस के अलावा	is ke alāva
that's why ...	इस लिए	is lie
in spite of ...	फिर भी ...	fir bhī ...
thanks to ...	... की मेहरबानी से	... kī meharabānī se
what (pron.)	क्या	kya
that (conj.)	कि	ki
something	कुछ	kuchh
anything (something)	कुछ भी	kuchh bhī
nothing	कुछ नहीं	kuchh nahin
who (pron.)	कौन	kaun
someone	कोई	koī
somebody	कोई	koī
nobody	कोई नहीं	koī nahin
nowhere (a voyage to ~)	कहीं नहीं	kahīn nahin
nobody's	किसी का नहीं	kisī ka nahin
somebody's	किसी का	kisī ka
so (I'm ~ glad)	कितना	kitana

also (as well)	भी	bhī
too (as well)	भी	bhī

6. Function words. Adverbs. Part 2

Why?	क्यों?	kyon?
for some reason	किसी कारणवश	kisī kāranavash
because ...	क्यों कि ...	kyon ki ...
for some purpose	किसी वजह से	kisī vajah se

and	और	aur
or	या	ya
but	लेकिन	lekin
for (e.g., ~ me)	के लिए	ke lie

too (~ many people)	ज़्यादा	zyāda
only (exclusively)	सिर्फ़	sirf
exactly (adv)	ठीक	thīk
about (more or less)	करीब	karīb

approximately (adv)	लगभग	lagabhag
approximate (adj)	अनुमानित	anumānit
almost (adv)	करीब	karīb
the rest	बाक़ी	bāqī

each (adj)	हर एक	har ek
any (no matter which)	कोई	koī
many, much (a lot of)	बहुत	bahut
many people	बहुत लोग	bahut log
all (everyone)	सभी	sabhī

in return for ...	... के बदले में	... ke badale men
in exchange (adv)	की जगह	kī jagah
by hand (made)	हाथ से	hāth se
hardly (negative opinion)	शायद ही	shāyad hī

probably (adv)	शायद	shāyad
on purpose (intentionally)	जानबूझकर	jānabūjhakar
by accident (adv)	संयोगवश	sanyogavash

very (adv)	बहुत	bahut
for example (adv)	उदाहरण के लिए	udāharan ke lie
between	के बीच	ke bīch
among	में	men
so much (such a lot)	इतना	itana
especially (adv)	ख़ासतौर पर	khāsataur par

NUMBERS. MISCELLANEOUS

7. Cardinal numbers. Part 1

0 zero	ज़ीरो	zīro
1 one	एक	ek
2 two	दो	do
3 three	तीन	tīn
4 four	चार	chār
5 five	पाँच	pānch
6 six	छह	chhah
7 seven	सात	sāt
8 eight	आठ	āth
9 nine	नौ	nau
10 ten	दस	das
11 eleven	ग्यारह	gyārah
12 twelve	बारह	bārah
13 thirteen	तेरह	terah
14 fourteen	चौदह	chaudah
15 fifteen	पन्द्रह	pandrah
16 sixteen	सोलह	solah
17 seventeen	सत्रह	satrah
18 eighteen	अठारह	athārah
19 nineteen	उन्नीस	unnīs
20 twenty	बीस	bīs
21 twenty-one	इक्कीस	ikkīs
22 twenty-two	बाईस	baīs
23 twenty-three	तेईस	teīs
30 thirty	तीस	tīs
31 thirty-one	इकतीस	ikattīs
32 thirty-two	बत्तीस	battīs
33 thirty-three	तैंतीस	taintīs
40 forty	चालीस	chālīs
41 forty-one	इक्तालीस	iktālīs
42 forty-two	बयालीस	bayālīs
43 forty-three	तैंतालीस	taintālīs
50 fifty	पचास	pachās
51 fifty-one	इक्यावन	ikyāvan
52 fifty-two	बावन	bāvan

53 fifty-three	तिरपन	tirapan
60 sixty	साठ	sāth
61 sixty-one	इकसठ	ikasath
62 sixty-two	बासठ	bāsath
63 sixty-three	तिरसठ	tirasath
70 seventy	सत्तर	sattar
71 seventy-one	इकहत्तर	ikahattar
72 seventy-two	बहत्तर	bahattar
73 seventy-three	तिहत्तर	tihattar
80 eighty	अस्सी	assī
81 eighty-one	इक्यासी	ikyāsī
82 eighty-two	बयासी	bayāsī
83 eighty-three	तिरासी	tirāsī
90 ninety	नब्बे	nabbe
91 ninety-one	इक्यानवे	ikyānave
92 ninety-two	बानवे	bānave
93 ninety-three	तिरानवे	tirānave

8. Cardinal numbers. Part 2

100 one hundred	सौ	sau
200 two hundred	दो सौ	do sau
300 three hundred	तीन सौ	tīn sau
400 four hundred	चार सौ	chār sau
500 five hundred	पाँच सौ	pānch sau
600 six hundred	छह सौ	chhah sau
700 seven hundred	सात सो	sāt so
800 eight hundred	आठ सौ	āth sau
900 nine hundred	नौ सौ	nau sau
1000 one thousand	एक हज़ार	ek hazār
2000 two thousand	दो हज़ार	do hazār
3000 three thousand	तीन हज़ार	tīn hazār
10000 ten thousand	दस हज़ार	das hazār
one hundred thousand	एक लाख	ek lākh
million	दस लाख (m)	das lākh
billion	अरब (m)	arab

9. Ordinal numbers

first (adj)	पहला	pahala
second (adj)	दूसरा	dūsara
third (adj)	तीसरा	tīsara
fourth (adj)	चौथा	chautha

fifth (adj)	पाँचवाँ	pānchavān
sixth (adj)	छठा	chhatha
seventh (adj)	सातवाँ	sātavān
eighth (adj)	आठवाँ	āthavān
ninth (adj)	नौवाँ	nauvān
tenth (adj)	दसवाँ	dasavān

COLOURS. UNITS OF MEASUREMENT

10. Colors

color	रंग (m)	rang
shade (tint)	रंग (m)	rang
hue	रंग (m)	rang
rainbow	इन्द्रधनुष (f)	indradhanush
white (adj)	सफ़ेद	safed
black (adj)	काला	kāla
gray (adj)	धूसर	dhūsar
green (adj)	हरा	hara
yellow (adj)	पीला	pīla
red (adj)	लाल	lāl
blue (adj)	नीला	nīla
light blue (adj)	हल्का नीला	halka nīla
pink (adj)	गुलाबी	gulābī
orange (adj)	नारंगी	nārangī
violet (adj)	बैंगनी	bainganī
brown (adj)	भूरा	bhūra
golden (adj)	सुनहरा	sunahara
silvery (adj)	चांदी-जैसा	chāndī-jaisa
beige (adj)	हल्का भूरा	halka bhūra
cream (adj)	क्रीम	krīm
turquoise (adj)	फ़िरोज़ी	fīrozī
cherry red (adj)	चेरी जैसा लाल	cherī jaisa lāl
lilac (adj)	हल्का बैंगनी	halka bainganī
crimson (adj)	गहरा लाल	gahara lāl
light (adj)	हल्का	halka
dark (adj)	गहरा	gahara
bright, vivid (adj)	चमकीला	chamakīla
colored (pencils)	रंगीन	rangīn
color (e.g., ~ film)	रंगीन	rangīn
black-and-white (adj)	काला-सफ़ेद	kāla-safed
plain (one-colored)	एक रंग का	ek rang ka
multicolored (adj)	बहुरंगी	bahurangī

11. Units of measurement

weight	वज़न (m)	vazan
length	लम्बाई (f)	lambaī
width	चौड़ाई (f)	chauraī
height	ऊंचाई (f)	ūnchaī
depth	गहराई (f)	gaharaī
volume	घनत्व (f)	ghanatv
area	क्षेत्रफल (m)	kshetrafal

gram	ग्राम (m)	grām
milligram	मिलीग्राम (m)	milīgrām
kilogram	किलोग्राम (m)	kilogrām
ton	टन (m)	tan
pound	पौण्ड (m)	paund
ounce	औन्स (m)	auns

meter	मीटर (m)	mītar
millimeter	मिलीमीटर (m)	milīmītar
centimeter	सेंटीमीटर (m)	sentīmītar
kilometer	किलोमीटर (m)	kilomītar
mile	मील (m)	mīl

inch	इंच (m)	inch
foot	फुट (m)	fut
yard	गज (m)	gaj

| square meter | वर्ग मीटर (m) | varg mītar |
| hectare | हेक्टेयर (m) | hekteyar |

liter	लीटर (m)	lītar
degree	डिग्री (m)	digrī
volt	वोल्ट (m)	volt
ampere	ऐम्पेयर (m)	aimpeyar
horsepower	अश्व शक्ति (f)	ashv shakti

quantity	मात्रा (f)	mātra
a little bit of ...	कुछ ...	kuchh ...
half	आधा (m)	ādha

| dozen | दर्जन (m) | darjan |
| piece (item) | टुकड़ा (m) | tukara |

| size | माप (m) | māp |
| scale (map ~) | पैमाना (m) | paimāna |

minimal (adj)	न्यूनतम	nyūnatam
the smallest (adj)	सब से छोटा	sab se chhota
medium (adj)	मध्य	madhy
maximal (adj)	अधिकतम	adhikatam
the largest (adj)	सबसे बड़ा	sabase bara

12. Containers

canning jar (glass ~)	शीशी (f)	shīshī
can	डिब्बा (m)	dibba
bucket	बाल्टी (f)	bāltī
barrel	पीपा (m)	pīpa
wash basin (e.g., plastic ~)	चिलमची (f)	chilamachī
tank (100L water ~)	कुण्ड (m)	kund
hip flask	फ्लास्क (m)	flāsk
jerrycan	जेरिकैन (m)	jerikain
tank (e.g., tank car)	टंकी (f)	tankī
mug	मग (m)	mag
cup (of coffee, etc.)	प्याली (f)	pyālī
saucer	सॉसर (m)	sosar
glass (tumbler)	गिलास (m)	gilās
wine glass	वाइन गिलास (m)	vain gilās
stock pot (soup pot)	सॉसपैन (m)	sosapain
bottle (~ of wine)	बोतल (f)	botal
neck (of the bottle, etc.)	गला (m)	gala
carafe (decanter)	जग (m)	jag
pitcher	सुराही (f)	surāhī
vessel (container)	बरतन (m)	baratan
pot (crock, stoneware ~)	घड़ा (m)	ghara
vase	फूलदान (m)	fūladān
bottle (perfume ~)	शीशी (f)	shīshī
vial, small bottle	शीशी (f)	shīshī
tube (of toothpaste)	ट्यूब (m)	tyūb
sack (bag)	थैला (m)	thaila
bag (paper ~, plastic ~)	थैली (f)	thailī
pack (of cigarettes, etc.)	पैकेट (f)	paiket
box (e.g., shoebox)	डिब्बा (m)	dibba
crate	डिब्बा (m)	dibba
basket	टोकरी (f)	tokarī

MAIN VERBS

13. The most important verbs. Part 1

to advise (vt)	सलाह देना	salāh dena
to agree (say yes)	राज़ी होना	rāzī hona
to answer (vi, vt)	जवाब देना	javāb dena
to apologize (vi)	माफ़ी मांगना	māfī māngana
to arrive (vi)	पहुँचना	pahunchana
to ask (~ oneself)	पूछना	pūchhana
to ask (~ sb to do sth)	मांगना	māngana
to be (vi)	होना	hona
to be afraid	डरना	darana
to be hungry	भूख लगना	bhūkh lagana
to be interested in ...	रुचि लेना	ruchi lena
to be needed	आवश्यक होना	āvashyak hona
to be surprised	हैरान होना	hairān hona
to be thirsty	प्यास लगना	pyās lagana
to begin (vt)	शुरू करना	shurū karana
to belong to ...	स्वामी होना	svāmī hona
to boast (vi)	डींग मारना	dīng mārana
to break (split into pieces)	तोड़ना	torana
to call (~ for help)	बुलाना	bulāna
can (v aux)	सकना	sakana
to catch (vt)	पकड़ना	pakarana
to change (vt)	बदलना	badalana
to choose (select)	चुनना	chunana
to come down (the stairs)	उतरना	utarana
to compare (vt)	तुलना करना	tulana karana
to complain (vi, vt)	शिकायत करना	shikāyat karana
to confuse (mix up)	गड़बड़ा जाना	garabara jāna
to continue (vt)	जारी रखना	jārī rakhana
to control (vt)	नियंत्रित करना	niyantrit karana
to cook (dinner)	खाना बनाना	khāna banāna
to cost (vt)	दाम होना	dām hona
to count (add up)	गिनना	ginana
to count on ...	भरोसा रखना	bharosa rakhana
to create (vt)	बनाना	banāna
to cry (weep)	रोना	rona

14. The most important verbs. Part 2

to deceive (vi, vt)	धोखा देना	dhokha dena
to decorate (tree, street)	सजाना	sajāna
to defend (a country, etc.)	रक्षा करना	raksha karana
to demand (request firmly)	माँगना	māngana
to dig (vt)	खोदना	khodana
to discuss (vt)	चर्चा करना	charcha karana
to do (vt)	करना	karana
to doubt (have doubts)	शक करना	shak karana
to drop (let fall)	गिराना	girāna
to enter (room, house, etc.)	अंदर आना	andar āna
to exist (vi)	होना	hona
to expect (foresee)	उम्मीद करना	ummīd karana
to explain (vt)	समझाना	samajhāna
to fall (vi)	गिरना	girana
to find (vt)	ढूँढना	dhūrhana
to finish (vt)	खत्म करना	khatm karana
to fly (vi)	उड़ना	urana
to follow ... (come after)	पीछे चलना	pīchhe chalana
to forget (vi, vt)	भूलना	bhūlana
to forgive (vt)	क्षमा करना	kshama karana
to give (vt)	देना	dena
to give a hint	इशारा करना	ishāra karana
to go (on foot)	जाना	jāna
to go for a swim	तैरना	tairana
to go out (for dinner, etc.)	बाहर जाना	bāhar jāna
to guess (the answer)	अंदाज़ा लगाना	andāza lagāna
to have (vt)	होना	hona
to have breakfast	नाश्ता करना	nāshta karana
to have dinner	रात्रिभोज करना	rātribhoj karana
to have lunch	दोपहर का भोजन करना	dopahar ka bhojan karana
to hear (vt)	सुनना	sunana
to help (vt)	मदद करना	madad karana
to hide (vt)	छिपाना	chhipāna
to hope (vi, vt)	आशा करना	āsha karana
to hunt (vi, vt)	शिकार करना	shikār karana
to hurry (vi)	जल्दी करना	jaldī karana

15. The most important verbs. Part 3

to inform (vt)	खबर देना	khabar dena
to insist (vi, vt)	आग्रह करना	āgrah karana

to insult (vt)	अपमान करना	apamān karana
to invite (vt)	आमंत्रित करना	āmantrit karana
to joke (vi)	मज़ाक करना	mazāk karana
to keep (vt)	रखना	rakhana
to keep silent	चुप रहना	chup rahana
to kill (vt)	मार डालना	mār dālana
to know (sb)	जानना	jānana
to know (sth)	मालूम होना	mālūm hona
to laugh (vi)	हंसना	hansana
to liberate (city, etc.)	आज़ाद करना	āzād karana
to like (I like …)	पसंद करना	pasand karana
to look for … (search)	तलाश करना	talāsh karana
to love (sb)	प्यार करना	pyār karana
to make a mistake	गलती करना	galatī karana
to manage, to run	प्रबंधन करना	prabandhan karana
to mean (signify)	अर्थ होना	arth hona
to mention (talk about)	उल्लेख करना	ullekh karana
to miss (school, etc.)	ग़ैर-हाज़िर होना	gair-hāzir hona
to notice (see)	देखना	dekhana
to object (vi, vt)	एतराज़ करना	etarāz karana
to observe (see)	देखना	dekhana
to open (vt)	खोलना	kholana
to order (meal, etc.)	ऑर्डर करना	ordar karana
to order (mil.)	हुक्म देना	hukm dena
to own (possess)	मालिक होना	mālik hona
to participate (vi)	भाग लेना	bhāg lena
to pay (vi, vt)	दाम चुकाना	dām chukāna
to permit (vt)	अनुमति देना	anumati dena
to plan (vt)	योजना बनाना	yojana banāna
to play (children)	खेलना	khelana
to pray (vi, vt)	दुआ देना	dua dena
to prefer (vt)	तरजीह देना	tarajīh dena
to promise (vt)	वचन देना	vachan dena
to pronounce (vt)	उच्चारण करना	uchchāran karana
to propose (vt)	प्रस्ताव रखना	prastāv rakhana
to punish (vt)	सज़ा देना	saza dena

16. The most important verbs. Part 4

to read (vi, vt)	पढ़ना	parhana
to recommend (vt)	सिफ़ारिश करना	sifārish karana
to refuse (vi, vt)	इन्कार करना	inkār karana
to regret (be sorry)	अफ़सोस जताना	afasos jatāna
to rent (sth from sb)	किराए पर लेना	kirae par lena

to repeat (say again)	दोहराना	doharāna
to reserve, to book	बुक करना	buk karana
to run (vi)	दौड़ना	daurana
to save (rescue)	बचाना	bachāna
to say (~ thank you)	कहना	kahana
to scold (vt)	डाँटना	dāntana
to see (vt)	देखना	dekhana
to sell (vt)	बेचना	bechana
to send (vt)	भेजना	bhejana
to shoot (vi)	गोली चलाना	golī chalāna
to shout (vi)	चिल्लाना	chillāna
to show (vt)	दिखाना	dikhāna
to sign (document)	हस्ताक्षर करना	hastākshar karana
to sit down (vi)	बैठना	baithana
to smile (vi)	मुस्कुराना	muskurāna
to speak (vi, vt)	बोलना	bolana
to steal (money, etc.)	चुराना	churāna
to stop (for pause, etc.)	रुकना	rukana
to stop (please ~ calling me)	बंद करना	band karana
to study (vt)	पढ़ाई करना	parhaī karana
to swim (vi)	तैरना	tairana
to take (vt)	लेना	lena
to think (vi, vt)	सोचना	sochana
to threaten (vt)	धमकाना	dhamakāna
to touch (with hands)	छूना	chhūna
to translate (vt)	अनुवाद करना	anuvād karana
to trust (vt)	यकीन करना	yakīn karana
to try (attempt)	कोशिश करना	koshish karana
to turn (e.g., ~ left)	मुड़ जाना	mur jāna
to underestimate (vt)	कम मूल्यांकन करना	kam mūlyānkan karana
to understand (vt)	समझना	samajhana
to unite (vt)	संयुक्त करना	sanyukt karana
to wait (vt)	इंतज़ार करना	intazār karana
to want (wish, desire)	चाहना	chāhana
to warn (vt)	चेतावनी देना	chetāvanī dena
to work (vi)	काम करना	kām karana
to write (vt)	लिखना	likhana
to write down	लिख लेना	likh lena

TIME. CALENDAR

17. Weekdays

Monday	सोमवार (m)	somavār
Tuesday	मंगलवार (m)	mangalavār
Wednesday	बुधवार (m)	budhavār
Thursday	गुरूवार (m)	gurūvār
Friday	शुक्रवार (m)	shukravār
Saturday	शनिवार (m)	shanivār
Sunday	रविवार (m)	ravivār
today (adv)	आज	āj
tomorrow (adv)	कल	kal
the day after tomorrow	परसों	parason
yesterday (adv)	कल	kal
the day before yesterday	परसों	parason
day	दिन (m)	din
working day	कार्यदिवस (m)	kāryadivas
public holiday	सार्वजनिक छुट्टी (f)	sārvajanik chhuttī
day off	छुट्टी का दिन (m)	chhuttī ka din
weekend	सप्ताहांत (m)	saptāhānt
all day long	सारा दिन	sāra din
the next day (adv)	अगला दिन	agala din
two days ago	दो दिन पहले	do din pahale
the day before	एक दिन पहले	ek din pahale
daily (adj)	दैनिक	dainik
every day (adv)	हर दिन	har din
week	हफ़ता (f)	hafata
last week (adv)	पिछले हफ़्ते	pichhale hafate
next week (adv)	अगले हफ़्ते	agale hafate
weekly (adj)	सप्ताहिक	saptāhik
every week (adv)	हर हफ़्ते	har hafate
twice a week	हफ़्ते में दो बार	hafate men do bār
every Tuesday	हर मंगलवार को	har mangalavār ko

18. Hours. Day and night

morning	सुबह (m)	subah
in the morning	सुबह में	subah men
noon, midday	दोपहर (m)	dopahar

in the afternoon	दोपहर में	dopahar men
evening	शाम (m)	shām
in the evening	शाम में	shām men
night	रात (f)	rāt
at night	रात में	rāt men
midnight	आधी रात (f)	ādhī rāt

second	सेकन्ड (m)	sekand
minute	मिनट (m)	minat
hour	घंटा (m)	ghanta
half an hour	आधा घंटा	ādha ghanta
a quarter-hour	सवा	sava
fifteen minutes	पंद्रह मीनट	pandrah mīnat
24 hours	24 घंटे (m)	chaubīs ghante

sunrise	सूर्यीदय (m)	sūryoday
dawn	सूर्यीदय (m)	sūryoday
early morning	प्रातःकाल (m)	prātahkāl
sunset	सूर्यास्त (m)	sūryāst

early in the morning	सुबह-सवेरे	subah-savere
this morning	इस सुबह	is subah
tomorrow morning	कल सुबह	kal subah

this afternoon	आज शाम	āj shām
in the afternoon	दोपहर में	dopahar men
tomorrow afternoon	कल दोपहर	kal dopahar

| tonight (this evening) | आज शाम | āj shām |
| tomorrow night | कल रात | kal rāt |

at 3 o'clock sharp	ठीक तीन बजे में	thīk tīn baje men
about 4 o'clock	लगभग चार बजे	lagabhag chār baje
by 12 o'clock	बारह बजे तक	bārah baje tak

in 20 minutes	बीस मीनट में	bīs mīnat men
in an hour	एक घंटे में	ek ghante men
on time (adv)	ठीक समय पर	thīk samay par

a quarter of ...	पौने ... बजे	paune ... baje
within an hour	एक घंटे के अंदर	ek ghante ke andar
every 15 minutes	हर पंद्रह मीनट	har pandrah mīnat
round the clock	दिन-रात (m pl)	din-rāt

19. Months. Seasons

January	जनवरी (m)	janavarī
February	फ़रवरी (m)	faravarī
March	मार्च (m)	mārch
April	अप्रैल (m)	aprail

May	माई (m)	maī
June	जून (m)	jūn
July	जुलाई (m)	julaī
August	अगस्त (m)	agast
September	सितम्बर (m)	sitambar
October	अक्तूबर (m)	aktūbar
November	नवम्बर (m)	navambar
December	दिसम्बर (m)	disambar
spring	वसन्त (m)	vasant
in spring	वसन्त में	vasant men
spring (as adj)	वसन्त	vasant
summer	गरमी (f)	garamī
in summer	गरमियों में	garamiyon men
summer (as adj)	गरमी	garamī
fall	शरद (m)	sharad
in fall	शरद में	sharad men
fall (as adj)	शरद	sharad
winter	सर्दी (f)	sardī
in winter	सर्दियों में	sardiyon men
winter (as adj)	सर्दी	sardī
month	महीना (m)	mahīna
this month	इस महीने	is mahīne
next month	अगले महीने	agale mahīne
last month	पिछले महीने	pichhale mahīne
a month ago	एक महीने पहले	ek mahīne pahale
in a month (a month later)	एक महीने में	ek mahīne men
in 2 months (2 months later)	दो महीने में	do mahīne men
the whole month	पूरे महीने	pūre mahīne
all month long	पूरे महीने	pūre mahīne
monthly (~ magazine)	मासिक	māsik
monthly (adv)	हर महीने	har mahīne
every month	हर महीने	har mahīne
twice a month	महिने में दो बार	mahine men do bār
year	वर्ष (m)	varsh
this year	इस साल	is sāl
next year	अगले साल	agale sāl
last year	पिछले साल	pichhale sāl
a year ago	एक साल पहले	ek sāl pahale
in a year	एक साल में	ek sāl men
in two years	दो साल में	do sāl men
the whole year	पूरा साल	pūra sāl

all year long	पूरा साल	pūra sāl
every year	हर साल	har sāl
annual (adj)	वार्षिक	vārshik
annually (adv)	वार्षिक	vārshik
4 times a year	साल में चार बार	sāl men chār bār
date (e.g., today's ~)	तारीख़ (f)	tārīkh
date (e.g., ~ of birth)	तारीख़ (f)	tārīkh
calendar	कैलेन्डर (m)	kailendar
half a year	आधे वर्ष (m)	ādhe varsh
six months	छमाही (f)	chhamāhī
season (summer, etc.)	मौसम (m)	mausam
century	शताबदी (f)	shatābadī

TRAVEL. HOTEL

20. Trip. Travel

tourism, travel	पर्यटन (m)	paryatan
tourist	पर्यटक (m)	paryatak
trip, voyage	यात्रा (f)	yātra
adventure	जाँबाज़ी (f)	jānbāzī
trip, journey	यात्रा (f)	yātra
vacation	छुट्टी (f)	chhuttī
to be on vacation	छुट्टी पर होना	chhuttī par hona
rest	आराम (m)	ārām
train	रेलगाड़ी, ट्रेन (f)	relagārī, tren
by train	रैलगाड़ी से	railagārī se
airplane	विमान (m)	vimān
by airplane	विमान से	vimān se
by car	कार से	kār se
by ship	जहाज़ पर	jahāz par
luggage	सामान (m)	sāmān
suitcase	सूटकेस (m)	sūtakes
luggage cart	सामान के लिये गाड़ी (f)	sāmān ke liye gārī
passport	पासपोर्ट (m)	pāsaport
visa	वीज़ा (m)	vīza
ticket	टिकट (m)	tikat
air ticket	हवाई टिकट (m)	havaī tikat
guidebook	गाइडबुक (f)	gaidabuk
map (tourist ~)	नक्शा (m)	naksha
area (rural ~)	क्षेत्र (m)	kshetr
place, site	स्थान (m)	sthān
exotica (n)	विचित्र वस्तुएं	vichitr vastuen
exotic (adj)	विचित्र	vichitr
amazing (adj)	अजीब	ajīb
group	समूह (m)	samūh
excursion, sightseeing tour	पर्यटन (f)	paryatan
guide (person)	गाइड (m)	gaid

21. Hotel

hotel	होटल (f)	hotal
motel	मोटल (m)	motal
three-star (~ hotel)	तीन सितारा	tīn sitāra
five-star	पाँच सितारा	pānch sitāra
to stay (in a hotel, etc.)	ठहरना	thaharana
room	कमरा (m)	kamara
single room	एक पलंग का कमरा (m)	ek palang ka kamara
double room	दो पलंगों का कमरा (m)	do palangon ka kamara
to book a room	कमरा बुक करना	kamara buk karana
half board	हाफ़-बोर्ड (m)	hāf-bord
full board	फ़ुल-बोर्ड (m)	ful-bord
with bath	स्नानघर के साथ	snānaghar ke sāth
with shower	शॉवर के साथ	shovar ke sāth
satellite television	सैटेलाइट टेलीविज़न (m)	saitelait telīvizan
air-conditioner	एयर-कंडिशनर (m)	eyar-kandishanar
towel	तौलिया (f)	tauliya
key	चाबी (f)	chābī
administrator	मैनेजर (m)	mainejar
chambermaid	चैमबरमैड (f)	chaimabaramaid
porter, bellboy	कुली (m)	kulī
doorman	दरबान (m)	darabān
restaurant	रेस्टराँ (m)	restarān
pub, bar	बार (m)	bār
breakfast	नाश्ता (m)	nāshta
dinner	रात्रिभोज (m)	rātribhoj
buffet	बुफ़े (m)	bufe
lobby	लॉबी (f)	lobī
elevator	लिफ़्ट (m)	lift
DO NOT DISTURB	परेशान न करें	pareshān na karen
NO SMOKING	धुम्रपान निषेध!	dhumrapān nishedh!

22. Sightseeing

monument	स्मारक (m)	smārak
fortress	किला (m)	kila
palace	भवन (m)	bhavan
castle	महल (m)	mahal
tower	मीनार (m)	mīnār
mausoleum	समाधि (f)	samādhi

architecture	वस्तुशाला (m)	vastushāla
medieval (adj)	मध्ययुगीय	madhayayugīy
ancient (adj)	प्राचीन	prāchīn
national (adj)	राष्ट्रीय	rāshtrīy
famous (monument, etc.)	मशहूर	mashhūr
tourist	पर्यटक (m)	paryatak
guide (person)	गाइड (m)	gaid
excursion, sightseeing tour	पर्यटन यात्रा (m)	paryatan yātra
to show (vt)	दिखाना	dikhāna
to tell (vt)	बताना	batāna
to find (vt)	ढूँढना	dhūnrhana
to get lost (lose one's way)	खो जाना	kho jāna
map (e.g., subway ~)	नक्शा (m)	naksha
map (e.g., city ~)	नक्शा (m)	naksha
souvenir, gift	यादगार (m)	yādagār
gift shop	गिफ्ट शॉप (f)	gift shop
to take pictures	फोटो खींचना	foto khīnchana
to have one's picture taken	अपना फ़ोटो खिंचवाना	apana foto khinchavāna

TRANSPORTATION

23. Airport

airport	हवाई अड्डा (m)	havaī adda
airplane	विमान (m)	vimān
airline	हवाई कम्पनी (f)	havaī kampanī
air traffic controller	हवाई यातायात नियंत्रक (m)	havaī yātāyāt niyantrak
departure	प्रस्थान (m)	prasthān
arrival	आगमन (m)	āgaman
to arrive (by plane)	पहुंचना	pahunchana
departure time	उड़ान का समय (m)	urān ka samay
arrival time	आगमन का समय (m)	āgaman ka samay
to be delayed	देर से आना	der se āna
flight delay	उड़ान देरी (f)	urān derī
information board	सूचना बोर्ड (m)	sūchana bord
information	सूचना (f)	sūchana
to announce (vt)	घोषणा करना	ghoshana karana
flight (e.g., next ~)	फ्लाइट (f)	flait
customs	सीमाशुल्क कार्यालय (m)	sīmāshulk kāryālay
customs officer	सीमाशुल्क अधिकारी (m)	sīmāshulk adhikārī
customs declaration	सीमाशुल्क घोषणा (f)	sīmāshulk ghoshana
to fill out the declaration	सीमाशुल्क घोषणा भरना	sīmāshulk ghoshana bharana
passport control	पासपोर्ट जांच (f)	pāsport jānch
luggage	सामान (m)	sāmān
hand luggage	दस्ती सामान (m)	dastī sāmān
luggage cart	सामान के लिये गाड़ी (f)	sāmān ke liye gārī
landing	विमानारोहण (m)	vimānārohan
landing strip	विमानारोहण मार्ग (m)	vimānārohan mārg
to land (vi)	उतरना	utarana
airstairs	सीढ़ी (f)	sīrhī
check-in	चेक-इन (m)	chek-in
check-in counter	चेक-इन डेस्क (m)	chek-in desk
to check-in (vi)	चेक-इन करना	chek-in karana

boarding pass	बोर्डिंग पास (m)	bording pās
departure gate	प्रस्थान गेट (m)	prasthān get
transit	पारवहन (m)	pāravahan
to wait (vt)	इंतज़ार करना	intazār karana
departure lounge	प्रतीक्षालय (m)	pratīkshālay
to see off	विदा करना	vida karana
to say goodbye	विदा कहना	vida kahana

24. Airplane

airplane	विमान (m)	vimān
air ticket	हवाई टिकट (m)	havaī tikat
airline	हवाई कम्पनी (f)	havaī kampanī
airport	हवाई अड्डा (m)	havaī adda
supersonic (adj)	पराध्वनिक	parādhvanik

captain	कसान (m)	kaptān
crew	वैमानिक दल (m)	vaimānik dal
pilot	विमान चालक (m)	vimān chālak
flight attendant (fem.)	एयर होस्टस (f)	eyar hostas
navigator	नैवीगेटर (m)	naivīgetar

wings	पंख (m pl)	pankh
tail	पूँछ (f)	pūnchh
cockpit	कॉकपिट (m)	kokapit
engine	इंजन (m)	injan
undercarriage (landing gear)	हवाई जहाज़ पहिये (m)	havaī jahāz pahiye
turbine	टरबाइन (f)	tarabain

propeller	प्रोपेलर (m)	propelar
black box	ब्लैक बॉक्स (m)	blaik boks
yoke (control column)	कंट्रोल कॉलम (m)	kantrol kolam
fuel	ईंधन (m)	īndhan

safety card	सुरक्षा-पत्र (m)	suraksha-patr
oxygen mask	ऑक्सीजन मास्क (m)	oksījan māsk
uniform	वर्दी (f)	vardī
life vest	बचाव पेटी (f)	bachāv petī
parachute	पैराशूट (m)	pairāshūt

takeoff	उड़ान (m)	urān
to take off (vi)	उड़ना	urana
runway	उड़ान पट्टी (f)	urān pattī
visibility	दृश्यता (f)	drshyata
flight (act of flying)	उड़ान (m)	urān
altitude	ऊंचाई (f)	ūnchaī
air pocket	वायु-पॉकेट (m)	vāyu-poket

| seat | सीट (f) | sīt |

headphones	हेडफ़ोन (m)	hedafon
folding tray (tray table)	ट्रे टेबल (f)	tre tebal
airplane window	हवाई जहाज़ की खिड़की (f)	havaī jahāz kī khirakī
aisle	गलियारा (m)	galiyāra

25. Train

train	रेलगाड़ी, ट्रेन (f)	relagārī, tren
commuter train	लोकल ट्रेन (f)	lokal tren
express train	तेज़ रेलगाड़ी (f)	tez relagārī
diesel locomotive	डीज़ल रेलगाड़ी (f)	dīzal relagārī
steam locomotive	स्टीम इंजन (f)	stīm injan
passenger car	कोच (f)	koch
dining car	डाइनर (f)	dainar
rails	पटरियाँ (f)	patariyān
railroad	रेलवे (f)	relave
railway tie	पटरियाँ (f)	patariyān
platform (railway ~)	प्लेटफॉर्म (m)	pletaform
track (~ 1, 2, etc.)	प्लेटफॉर्म (m)	pletaform
semaphore	सिग्नल (m)	signal
station	स्टेशन (m)	steshan
engineer (train driver)	इंजन ड्राइवर (m)	injan draivar
porter (of luggage)	कुली (m)	kulī
car attendant	कोच एटेंडेंट (m)	koch etendent
passenger	मुसाफ़िर (m)	musāfir
conductor	टीटी (m)	tītī
(ticket inspector)		
corridor (in train)	गलियारा (m)	galiyāra
emergency brake	आपात ब्रेक (m)	āpāt brek
compartment	डिब्बा (m)	dibba
berth	बर्थ (f)	barth
upper berth	ऊपरी बर्थ (f)	ūparī barth
lower berth	नीचली बर्थ (f)	nīchalī barth
bed linen, bedding	बिस्तर (m)	bistar
ticket	टिकट (m)	tikat
schedule	टाइम टैबुल (m)	taim taibul
information display	सूचना बोर्ड (m)	sūchana bord
to leave, to depart	चले जाना	chale jāna
departure (of train)	रवानगी (f)	ravānagī
to arrive (ab. train)	पहुंचना	pahunchana
arrival	आगमन (m)	āgaman
to arrive by train	गाड़ी से पहुंचना	gārī se pahunchana

to get on the train	गाड़ी पकड़ना	gādī pakarana
to get off the train	गाड़ी से उतरना	gārī se utarana
train wreck	दुर्घटनाग्रस्त (f)	durghatanāgrast
steam locomotive	स्टीम इंजन (m)	stīm injan
stoker, fireman	अग्निशामक (m)	agnishāmak
firebox	भट्ठी (f)	bhatthī
coal	कोयला (m)	koyala

26. Ship

| ship | जहाज़ (m) | jahāz |
| vessel | जहाज़ (m) | jahāz |

steamship	जहाज़ (m)	jahāz
riverboat	मोटर बोट (m)	motar bot
cruise ship	लाइनर (m)	lainar
cruiser	क्रूज़र (m)	krūzar

yacht	याख्ट (m)	yākht
tugboat	कर्षक पोत (m)	karshak pot
barge	बार्ज (f)	bārj
ferry	फेरी बोट (f)	ferī bot

| sailing ship | पाल नाव (f) | pāl nāv |
| brigantine | बादबानी (f) | bādabānī |

| ice breaker | हिमभंजक पोत (m) | himabhanjak pot |
| submarine | पनडुब्बी (f) | panadubbī |

boat (flat-bottomed ~)	नाव (m)	nāv
dinghy	किश्ती (f)	kishtī
lifeboat	जीवन रक्षा किश्ती (f)	jīvan raksha kishtī
motorboat	मोटर बोट (m)	motar bot

captain	कप्तान (m)	kaptān
seaman	मल्लाह (m)	mallāh
sailor	मल्लाह (m)	mallāh
crew	वैमानिक दल (m)	vaimānik dal

boatswain	बोसुन (m)	bosun
ship's boy	बोसुन (m)	bosun
cook	रसोइया (m)	rasoiya
ship's doctor	पोत डाक्टर (m)	pot dāktar

deck	डेक (m)	dek
mast	मस्तूल (m)	mastūl
sail	पाल (m)	pāl

| hold | कार्गी (m) | kārgo |
| bow (prow) | जहाज़ का अगड़ा हिस्सा (m) | jahāz ka agara hissa |

stern	जहाज़ का पिछला हिस्सा (m)	jahāz ka pichhala hissa
oar	चप्पू (m)	chappū
screw propeller	जहाज़ की पंखी चलाने का पेंच (m)	jahāz kī pankhī chalāne ka pench

cabin	कैबिन (m)	kaibin
wardroom	मेस (f)	mes
engine room	मशीन-कमरा (m)	mashīn-kamara
bridge	ब्रिज (m)	brij
radio room	रेडियो केबिन (m)	rediyo kebin
wave (radio)	रेडियो तरंग (f)	rediyo tarang
logbook	जहाज़ी रजिस्टर (m)	jahāzī rajistar

spyglass	टेलिस्कोप (m)	teliskop
bell	घंटा (m)	ghanta
flag	झंडा (m)	jhanda

| hawser (mooring ~) | रस्सा (m) | rassa |
| knot (bowline, etc.) | जहाज़ी गांठ (f) | jahāzī gānth |

| deckrails | रेलिंग (f) | reling |
| gangway | सीढ़ी (f) | sīrhī |

anchor	लंगर (m)	langar
to weigh anchor	लंगर उठाना	langar uthāna
to drop anchor	लंगर डालना	langar dālana
anchor chain	लंगर की ज़ंजीर (f)	langar kī zajīr

port (harbor)	बंदरगाह (m)	bandaragāh
quay, wharf	घाट (m)	ghāt
to berth (moor)	किनारे लगना	kināre lagana
to cast off	रवाना होना	ravāna hona

trip, voyage	यात्रा (f)	yātra
cruise (sea trip)	जलयात्रा (f)	jalayātra
course (route)	दिशा (f)	disha
route (itinerary)	मार्ग (m)	mārg

fairway (safe water channel)	नाव्य जलपथ (m)	nāvy jalapath
shallows	छिछला पानी (m)	chhichhala pānī
to run aground	छिछले पानी में धसना	chhichhale pānī men dhansana

storm	तूफ़ान (m)	tufān
signal	सिग्नल (m)	signal
to sink (vi)	डूबना	dūbana
SOS (distress signal)	एसओएस	esoes
ring buoy	लाइफ ब्वाय (m)	laif bvāy

CITY

27. Urban transportation

bus	बस (f)	bas
streetcar	ट्रैम (m)	traim
trolley bus	ट्रॉलीबस (f)	trolības
route (of bus, etc.)	मार्ग (m)	mārg
number (e.g., bus ~)	नम्बर (m)	nambar
to go by ...	के माध्यम से जाना	ke mādhyam se jāna
to get on (~ the bus)	सवार होना	savār hona
to get off ...	उतरना	utarana
stop (e.g., bus ~)	बस स्टॉप (m)	bas stop
next stop	अगला स्टॉप (m)	agala stop
terminus	अंतिम स्टेशन (m)	antim steshan
schedule	समय सारणी (f)	samay sāranī
to wait (vt)	इंतज़ार करना	intazār karana
ticket	टिकट (m)	tikat
fare	टिकट का किराया (m)	tikat ka kirāya
cashier (ticket seller)	कैशियर (m)	kaishiyar
ticket inspection	टिकट जाँच (f)	tikat jānch
ticket inspector	कंडक्टर (m)	kandaktar
to be late (for ...)	देर हो जाना	der ho jāna
to miss (~ the train, etc.)	छूट जाना	chhūt jāna
to be in a hurry	जल्दी में रहना	jaldī men rahana
taxi, cab	टैक्सी (m)	taiksī
taxi driver	टैक्सीवाला (m)	taiksīvāla
by taxi	टैक्सी से (m)	taiksī se
taxi stand	टैक्सी स्टैंड (m)	taiksī staind
to call a taxi	टैक्सी बुलाना	taiksī bulāna
to take a taxi	टैक्सी लेना	taiksī lena
traffic	यातायात (f)	yātāyāt
traffic jam	ट्रैफ़िक जाम (m)	traifik jām
rush hour	भीड़ का समय (m)	bhīr ka samay
to park (vi)	पार्क करना	pārk karana
to park (vt)	पार्क करना	pārk karana
parking lot	पार्किंग (f)	pārking
subway	मेट्रो (m)	metro
station	स्टेशन (m)	steshan

to take the subway	मेट्रो लेना	metro lena
train	रेलगाड़ी, ट्रेन (f)	relagārī, tren
train station	स्टेशन (m)	steshan

28. City. Life in the city

city, town	नगर (m)	nagar
capital city	राजधानी (f)	rājadhānī
village	गांव (m)	gānv

city map	नगर का नक्शा (m)	nagar ka naksha
downtown	नगर का केन्द्र (m)	nagar ka kendr
suburb	उपनगर (m)	upanagar
suburban (adj)	उपनगरिक	upanagarik

outskirts	बाहरी इलाका (m)	bāharī ilāka
environs (suburbs)	इर्दगिर्द के इलाके (m pl)	irdagird ke ilāke
city block	सेक्टर (m)	sektar
residential block (area)	मुहल्ला (m)	muhalla

traffic	यातायात (f)	yātāyāt
traffic lights	यातायात सिग्नल (m)	yātāyāt signal
public transportation	जन परिवहन (m)	jan parivahan
intersection	चौराहा (m)	chaurāha

crosswalk	ज़ेबरा क्रॉसिंग (f)	zebara krosing
pedestrian underpass	पैदल यात्रियों के लिए अंडरपास (f)	paidal yātriyon ke lie andarapās
to cross (~ the street)	सड़क पार करना	sarak pār karana
pedestrian	पैदल-यात्री (m)	paidal-yātrī
sidewalk	फुटपाथ (m)	futapāth

bridge	पुल (m)	pul
embankment (river walk)	तट (m)	tat
fountain	फौवारा (m)	fauvāra

allée (garden walkway)	छायापथ (f)	chhāyāpath
park	पार्क (m)	pārk
boulevard	चौड़ी सड़क (m)	chaurī sarak
square	मैदान (m)	maidān
avenue (wide street)	मार्ग (m)	mārg
street	सड़क (f)	sarak
side street	गली (f)	galī
dead end	बंद गली (f)	band galī

house	मकान (m)	makān
building	इमारत (f)	imārat
skyscraper	गगनचुंबी भवन (f)	gaganachumbī bhavan
facade	अगवाड़ा (m)	agavāra
roof	छत (f)	chhat

window	खिड़की (f)	khirakī
arch	मेहराब (m)	meharāb
column	स्तंभ (m)	stambh
corner	कोना (m)	kona

store window	दुकान का शो-केस (m)	dukān ka sho-kes
signboard (store sign, etc.)	साईनबोर्ड (m)	saīnabord
poster	पोस्टर (m)	postar
advertising poster	विज्ञापन पोस्टर (m)	vigyāpan postar
billboard	बिलबोर्ड (m)	bilabord

garbage, trash	कूड़ा (m)	kūra
trashcan (public ~)	कूड़े का डिब्बा (m)	kūre ka dibba
to litter (vi)	कूड़ा-कर्कट डालना	kūra-karkat dālana
garbage dump	डम्पिंग ग्राउंड (m)	damping graund

phone booth	फ़ोन बूथ (m)	fon būth
lamppost	बिजली का खंभा (m)	bijalī ka khambha
bench (park ~)	पार्क-बेंच (f)	pārk-bench

police officer	पुलिसवाला (m)	pulisavāla
police	पुलिस (m)	pulis
beggar	भिखारी (m)	bhikhārī
homeless (n)	बेघर (m)	beghar

29. Urban institutions

store	दुकान (f)	dukān
drugstore, pharmacy	दवाख़ाना (m)	davākhāna
eyeglass store	चश्मे की दुकान (f)	chashme kī dukān
shopping mall	शॉपिंग मॉल (m)	shoping mol
supermarket	सुपर बाज़ार (m)	supar bāzār

bakery	बेकरी (f)	bekarī
baker	बेकर (m)	bekar
pastry shop	टॉफ़ी की दुकान (f)	tofī kī dukān
grocery store	परचून की दुकान (f)	parachūn kī dukān
butcher shop	गोश्त की दुकान (f)	gosht kī dukān

| produce store | सब्ज़ियों की दुकान (f) | sabziyon kī dukān |
| market | बाज़ार (m) | bāzār |

coffee house	काफ़ी हाउस (m)	kāfī haus
restaurant	रेस्टराँ (m)	restarān
pub, bar	शराबख़ाना (m)	sharābakhāna
pizzeria	पिट्ज़ा की दुकान (f)	pitza kī dukān

hair salon	नाई की दुकान (f)	naī kī dukān
post office	डाकघर (m)	dākaghar
dry cleaners	ड्राइक्लीनर (m)	draiklīnar

photo studio	फ़ोटो की दुकान (f)	foto kī dukān
shoe store	जूते की दुकान (f)	jūte kī dukān
bookstore	किताबों की दुकान (f)	kitābon kī dukān
sporting goods store	खेलकूद की दुकान (f)	khelakūd kī dukān
clothes repair shop	कपड़ों की मरम्मत की दुकान (f)	kaparon kī marammat kī dukān
formal wear rental	कपड़ों को किराए पर देने की दुकान (f)	kaparon ko kirae par dene kī dukān
video rental store	वीडियो रेन्टल दुकान (f)	vīdiyo rental dukān
circus	सर्कस (m)	sarkas
zoo	चिड़ियाघर (m)	chiriyāghar
movie theater	सिनेमाघर (m)	sinemāghar
museum	संग्रहालय (m)	sangrahālay
library	पुस्तकालय (m)	pustakālay
theater	रंगमंच (m)	rangamanch
opera (opera house)	ओपेरा (m)	opera
nightclub	नाईट क्लब (m)	naīt klab
casino	केसिनो (m)	kesino
mosque	मस्जिद (m)	masjid
synagogue	सीनागोग (m)	sīnāgog
cathedral	गिरजाघर (m)	girajāghar
temple	मंदिर (m)	mandir
church	गिरजाघर (m)	girajāghar
college	कॉलेज (m)	kolej
university	विश्वविद्यालय (m)	vishvavidyālay
school	विद्यालय (m)	vidyālay
prefecture	प्रशासक प्रान्त (m)	prashāsak prānt
city hall	सिटी हॉल (m)	sitī hol
hotel	होटल (f)	hotal
bank	बैंक (m)	baink
embassy	दूतावस (m)	dūtāvas
travel agency	पर्यटन आफ़िस (m)	paryatan āfis
information office	पूछताछ कार्यालय (m)	pūchhatāchh kāryālay
currency exchange	मुद्रालय (m)	mudrālay
subway	मेट्रो (m)	metro
hospital	अस्पताल (m)	aspatāl
gas station	पेट्रोल पम्प (f)	petrol pamp
parking lot	पार्किंग (f)	pārking

30. Signs

signboard (store sign, etc.)	साईनबोर्ड (m)	saīnabord
notice (door sign, etc.)	दुकान का साईन (m)	dukān ka saīn

poster	पोस्टर (m)	postar
direction sign	दिशा संकेतक (m)	disha sanketak
arrow (sign)	तीर दिशा संकेतक (m)	tīr disha sanketak
caution	चेतावनी (f)	chetāvanī
warning sign	चेतावनी संकेतक (m)	chetāvanī sanketak
to warn (vt)	चेतावनी देना	chetāvanī dena
rest day (weekly ~)	छुट्टी का दिन (m)	chhuttī ka din
timetable (schedule)	समय सारणी (f)	samay sāranī
opening hours	खुलने का समय (m)	khulane ka samay
WELCOME!	आपका स्वागत है।	āpaka svāgat hai!
ENTRANCE	प्रवेश	pravesh
EXIT	निकास	nikās
PUSH	धक्का दें	dhakka den
PULL	खींचे	khīnche
OPEN	खुला	khula
CLOSED	बंद	band
WOMEN	औरतों के लिये	auraton ke liye
MEN	आदमियों के लिये	ādamiyon ke liye
DISCOUNTS	डिस्काउन्ट	diskaunt
SALE	सेल	sel
NEW!	नया!	naya!
FREE	मुफ्त	muft
ATTENTION!	ध्यान दें!	dhyān den!
NO VACANCIES	कोई जगह खाली नहीं है	koī jagah khālī nahin hai
RESERVED	रिज़र्वड	rizarvad
ADMINISTRATION	प्रशासन	prashāsan
STAFF ONLY	केवल कर्मचारियों के लिए	keval karmachāriyon ke lie
BEWARE OF THE DOG!	कुत्ते से सावधान!	kutte se sāvadhān!
NO SMOKING	धुम्रपान निषेध!	dhumrapān nishedh!
DO NOT TOUCH!	छूना मना!	chhūna mana!
DANGEROUS	खतरा	khatara
DANGER	खतरा	khatara
HIGH VOLTAGE	उच्च वोल्टेज	uchch voltej
NO SWIMMING!	तैरना मना!	tairana mana!
OUT OF ORDER	ख़राब	kharāb
FLAMMABLE	ज्वलनशील	jvalanashīl
FORBIDDEN	निषिद्ध	nishiddh
NO TRESPASSING!	प्रवेश निषेध!	pravesh nishedh!
WET PAINT	गीला पेंट	gīla pent

31. Shopping

to buy (purchase)	खरीदना	kharīdana
purchase	खरीदारी (f)	kharīdārī
to go shopping	खरीदारी करने जाना	kharīdārī karane jāna
shopping	खरीदारी (f)	kharīdārī
to be open (ab. store)	खुला होना	khula hona
to be closed	बन्द होना	band hona
footwear, shoes	जूता (m)	jūta
clothes, clothing	पोशाक (m)	poshāk
cosmetics	श्रृंगार-सामग्री (f)	shrrngār-sāmagrī
food products	खाने-पीने की चीज़ें (f pl)	khāne-pīne kī chīzen
gift, present	उपहार (m)	upahār
salesman	बेचनेवाला (m)	bechanevāla
saleswoman	बेचनेवाली (f)	bechanevālī
check out, cash desk	कैश-काउन्टर (m)	kaish-kauntar
mirror	आईना (m)	āīna
counter (store ~)	काउन्टर (m)	kauntar
fitting room	ट्राई करने का कमरा (m)	traī karane ka kamara
to try on	ट्राई करना	traī karana
to fit (ab. dress, etc.)	फिटिंग करना	fiting karana
to like (I like …)	पसंद करना	pasand karana
price	दाम (m)	dām
price tag	प्राइस टैग (m)	prais taig
to cost (vt)	दाम होना	dām hona
How much?	कितना?	kitana?
discount	डिस्काउन्ट (m)	diskaunt
inexpensive (adj)	सस्ता	sasta
cheap (adj)	सस्ता	sasta
expensive (adj)	महंगा	mahanga
It's expensive	यह महंगा है	yah mahanga hai
rental (n)	रेन्टल (m)	rental
to rent (~ a tuxedo)	किराए पर लेना	kirae par lena
credit (trade credit)	क्रेडिट (m)	kredit
on credit (adv)	क्रेडिट पर	kredit par

CLOTHING & ACCESSORIES

32. Outerwear. Coats

clothes	कपड़े (m)	kapare
outerwear	बाहरी पोशाक (m)	bāharī poshāk
winter clothing	सर्दियों की पोशक (f)	sardiyon kī poshak
coat (overcoat)	ओवरकोट (m)	ovarakot
fur coat	फरकोट (m)	farakot
fur jacket	फ़र की जैकेट (f)	far kī jaiket
down coat	फ़ेदर कोट (m)	fedar kot
jacket (e.g., leather ~)	जैकेट (f)	jaiket
raincoat (trenchcoat, etc.)	बरसाती (f)	barasātī
waterproof (adj)	जलरोधक	jalarodhak

33. Men's & women's clothing

shirt (button shirt)	कमीज़ (f)	kamīz
pants	पैंट (m)	paint
jeans	जीन्स (m)	jīns
suit jacket	कोट (m)	kot
suit	सूट (m)	sūt
dress (frock)	फ़ॉक (f)	frok
skirt	स्कर्ट (f)	skart
blouse	ब्लाउज़ (f)	blauz
knitted jacket (cardigan, etc.)	कार्डिगन (f)	kārdigan
jacket (of woman's suit)	जैकेट (f)	jaiket
T-shirt	टी-शर्ट (f)	tī-shart
shorts (short trousers)	शोर्ट्स (m pl)	shorts
tracksuit	ट्रैक सूट (m)	traik sūt
bathrobe	बाथ रोब (m)	bāth rob
pajamas	पजामा (m)	pajāma
sweater	सूटर (m)	sūtar
pullover	पुलोवर (m)	pulovar
vest	बण्डी (m)	bandī
tailcoat	टेल-कोट (m)	tel-kot
tuxedo	डिनर-जैकेट (f)	dinar-jaiket

uniform	वर्दी (f)	vardī
workwear	वर्दी (f)	vardī
overalls	ओवरऑल्स (m)	ovarols
coat (e.g., doctor's smock)	कोट (m)	kot

34. Clothing. Underwear

underwear	अंगवस्त्र (m)	angavastr
undershirt (A-shirt)	बनियान (f)	baniyān
socks	मोज़े (m pl)	moze

nightgown	नाइट गाउन (m)	nait gaun
bra	ब्रा (f)	bra
knee highs (knee-high socks)	घुटनों तक के मोज़े (m)	ghutanon tak ke moze
pantyhose	टाइट्स (m pl)	taits
stockings (thigh highs)	स्टॉकिंग (m pl)	stāking
bathing suit	स्विम सूट (m)	svim sūt

35. Headwear

hat	टोपी (f)	topī
fedora	हैट (f)	hait
baseball cap	बैस्बॉल कैप (f)	baisbol kaip
flatcap	फ़्लैट कैप (f)	flait kaip

beret	बेरेट (m)	beret
hood	हूड (m)	hūd
panama hat	पनामा हैट (m)	panāma hait
knit cap (knitted hat)	बुनी हुई टोपी (f)	bunī huī topī

| headscarf | सिर का स्कार्फ़ (m) | sir ka skārf |
| women's hat | महिलाओं की टोपी (f) | mahilaon kī topī |

hard hat	हेलमेट (f)	helamet
garrison cap	पुलिसीया टोपी (f)	pulisīya topī
helmet	हेलमेट (f)	helamet

| derby | बॉलर हैट (m) | bolar hait |
| top hat | टॉप हैट (m) | top hait |

36. Footwear

footwear	पनही (f)	panahī
shoes (men's shoes)	जूते (m pl)	jūte
shoes (women's shoes)	जूते (m pl)	jūte

boots (e.g., cowboy ~)	बूट (m pl)	būt
slippers	चप्पल (f pl)	chappal
tennis shoes (e.g., Nike ~)	टेनिस के जूते (m)	tenis ke jūte
sneakers (e.g., Converse ~)	स्नीकर्स (m)	snīkars
sandals	सैन्डल (f)	saindal
cobbler (shoe repairer)	मोची (m)	mochī
heel	एड़ी (f)	erī
pair (of shoes)	जोड़ा (m)	jora
shoestring	जूते का फ़ीता (m)	jūte ka fīta
to lace (vt)	फ़ीता बाँधना	fīta bāndhana
shoehorn	शू-होर्न (m)	shū-horn
shoe polish	बूट-पालिश (m)	būt-pālish

37. Personal accessories

gloves	दस्ताने (m pl)	dastāne
mittens	दस्ताने (m pl)	dastāne
scarf (muffler)	मफ़लर (m)	mafalar
glasses (eyeglasses)	ऐनक (m pl)	ainak
frame (eyeglass ~)	चश्मे का फ्रेम (m)	chashme ka frem
umbrella	छतरी (f)	chhatarī
walking stick	छड़ी (f)	chharī
hairbrush	ब्रश (m)	brash
fan	पंखा (m)	pankha
tie (necktie)	टाई (f)	taī
bow tie	बो टाई (f)	bo taī
suspenders	पतलून बाँधने का फ़ीता (m)	patalūn bāndhane ka fīta
handkerchief	रूमाल (m)	rūmāl
comb	कंघा (m)	kangha
barrette	बालपिन (f)	bālapin
hairpin	हेयरक्लीप (f)	heyaraklīp
buckle	बकसुआ (m)	bakasua
belt	बेल्ट (m)	belt
shoulder strap	कंधे का पट्टा (m)	kandhe ka patta
bag (handbag)	बैग (m)	baig
purse	पर्स (m)	pars
backpack	बैकपैक (m)	baikapaik

38. Clothing. Miscellaneous

fashion	फ़ैशन (m)	faishan
in vogue (adj)	प्रचलन में	prachalan men
fashion designer	फ़ैशन डिज़ाइनर (m)	faishan dizainar
collar	कॉलर (m)	kolar
pocket	जेब (m)	jeb
pocket (as adj)	जेब	jeb
sleeve	आस्तीन (f)	āstīn
hanging loop	हैंगिंग लूप (f)	hainging lūp
fly (on trousers)	ज़िप (f)	zip
zipper (fastener)	ज़िप (f)	zip
fastener	हुक (m)	huk
button	बटन (m)	batan
buttonhole	बटन का काज (m)	batan ka kāj
to come off (ab. button)	निकल जाना	nikal jāna
to sew (vi, vt)	सीना	sīna
to embroider (vi, vt)	काढ़ना	kārhana
embroidery	कढ़ाई (f)	karhaī
sewing needle	सूई (f)	sūī
thread	धागा (m)	dhāga
seam	सीवन (m)	sīvan
to get dirty (vi)	मैला होना	maila hona
stain (mark, spot)	धब्बा (m)	dhabba
to crease, crumple (vi)	शिकन पड़ जाना	shikan par jāna
to tear, to rip (vt)	फट जाना	fat jāna
clothes moth	कपड़ों के कीड़े (m)	kaparon ke kīre

39. Personal care. Cosmetics

toothpaste	टूथपेस्ट (m)	tūthapest
toothbrush	टूथब्रश (m)	tūthabrash
to brush one's teeth	दाँत साफ़ करना	dānt sāf karana
razor	रेज़र (f)	rezar
shaving cream	हजामत का क्रीम (m)	hajāmat ka krīm
to shave (vi)	शेव करना	shev karana
soap	साबुन (m)	sābun
shampoo	शैम्पू (m)	shaimpū
scissors	कैंची (f pl)	kainchī
nail file	नाख़ून घिसनी (f)	nākhūn ghisanī
nail clippers	नाख़ून कतरनी (f)	nākhūn kataranī
tweezers	ट्वीज़र्स (f)	tvīzars

cosmetics	श्रृंगार-सामग्री (f)	shrrngār-sāmagrī
face mask	चेहरे का लेप (m)	chehare ka lep
manicure	मैनीक्योर (m)	mainīkyor
to have a manicure	मैनीक्योर करवाना	mainīkyor karavāna
pedicure	पेडिक्यूर (m)	pedikyūr

make-up bag	श्रृंगार थैली (f)	shrrngār thailī
face powder	पाउडर (m)	paudar
powder compact	कॉम्पैक्ट पाउडर (m)	kompaikt paudar
blusher	ब्लशर (m)	blashar

perfume (bottled)	खुशबू (f)	khushabū
toilet water (lotion)	टॉयलेट वॉटर (m)	tāyalet votar
lotion	लोशन (m)	loshan
cologne	कोलोन (m)	kolon

eyeshadow	आई-शैडो (m)	āī-shaido
eyeliner	आई-पेंसिल (f)	āī-pensil
mascara	मस्कारा (m)	maskāra

lipstick	लिपस्टिक (m)	lipastik
nail polish, enamel	नेल पॉलिश (f)	nel polish
hair spray	हेयर स्प्रे (m)	heyar spre
deodorant	डिओडरेन्ट (m)	diodarent

cream	क्रीम (m)	krīm
face cream	चेहरे की क्रीम (f)	chehare kī krīm
hand cream	हाथ की क्रीम (f)	hāth kī krīm
anti-wrinkle cream	एंटी रिंकल क्रीम (f)	entī rinkal krīm
day (as adj)	दिन का	din ka
night (as adj)	रात का	rāt ka

tampon	टैम्पन (m)	taimpan
toilet paper (toilet roll)	टॉयलेट पेपर (m)	toyalet pepar
hair dryer	हेयर ड्रायर (m)	heyar drāyar

40. Watches. Clocks

watch (wristwatch)	घड़ी (f pl)	gharī
dial	डायल (m)	dāyal
hand (of clock, watch)	सुई (f)	suī
metal watch band	धातु से बनी घड़ी का पट्टा (m)	dhātu se banī gharī ka patta
watch strap	घड़ी का पट्टा (m)	gharī ka patta

battery	बैटरी (f)	baiterī
to be dead (battery)	ख़त्म हो जाना	khatm ho jāna
to change a battery	बैटरी बदलना	baiterī badalana
to run fast	तेज़ चलना	tez chalana
to run slow	धीमी चलना	dhīmī chalana

wall clock	दीवार-घड़ी (f pl)	dīvār-gharī
hourglass	रेत-घड़ी (f pl)	ret-gharī
sundial	सूरज-घड़ी (f pl)	sūraj-gharī
alarm clock	अलार्म घड़ी (f)	alārm gharī
watchmaker	घड़ीसाज़ (m)	gharīsāz
to repair (vt)	मरम्मत करना	marammat karana

EVERYDAY EXPERIENCE

41. Money

money	पैसा (m pl)	paisa
currency exchange	मुद्रा विनिमय (m)	mudra vinimay
exchange rate	विनिमय दर (m)	vinimay dar
ATM	एटीएम (m)	etīem
coin	सिक्का (m)	sikka
dollar	डॉलर (m)	dolar
euro	यूरो (m)	yūro
lira	लीरा (f)	līra
Deutschmark	डचमार्क (m)	dachamārk
franc	फ्रांक (m)	frānk
pound sterling	पाउन्ड स्टरलिंग (m)	paund staraling
yen	येन (m)	yen
debt	कर्ज़ (m)	karz
debtor	क़र्ज़दार (m)	qarzadār
to lend (money)	कर्ज़ देना	karz dena
to borrow (vi, vt)	कर्ज़ लेना	karz lena
bank	बैंक (m)	baink
account	बैंक खाता (m)	baink khāta
to deposit into the account	बैंक खाते में जमा करना	baink khāte men jama karana
to withdraw (vt)	खाते से पैसे निकालना	khāte se paise nikālana
credit card	क्रेडिट कार्ड (m)	kredit kārd
cash	कैश (m pl)	kaish
check	चेक (m)	chek
to write a check	चेक लिखना	chek likhana
checkbook	चेकबुक (f)	chekabuk
wallet	बटुआ (m)	batua
change purse	बटुआ (m)	batua
safe	लॉकर (m)	lokar
heir	उत्तराधिकारी (m)	uttarādhikārī
inheritance	उत्तराधिकार (m)	uttarādhikār
fortune (wealth)	संपत्ति (f)	sampatti
lease	किराये पर देना (m)	kirāye par dena
rent (money)	किराया (m)	kirāya

to rent (sth from sb)	किराए पर लेना	kirae par lena
price	दाम (m)	dām
cost	कीमत (f)	kīmat
sum	रक़म (m)	raqam

to spend (vt)	खर्च करना	kharch karana
expenses	खर्च (m pl)	kharch
to economize (vi, vt)	बचत करना	bachat karana
economical	किफ़ायती	kifāyatī

to pay (vi, vt)	दाम चुकाना	dām chukāna
payment	भुगतान (m)	bhugatān
change (give the ~)	चिल्लर (m)	chillar

tax	टैक्स (m)	taiks
fine	जुर्माना (m)	jurmāna
to fine (vt)	जुर्माना लगाना	jurmāna lagāna

42. Post. Postal service

post office	डाकघर (m)	dākaghar
mail (letters, etc.)	डाक (m)	dāk
mailman	डाकिया (m)	dākiya
opening hours	खुलने का समय (m)	khulane ka samay

letter	पत्र (m)	patr
registered letter	रजिस्टरी पत्र (m)	rajistarī patr
postcard	पोस्ट कार्ड (m)	post kārd
telegram	तार (m)	tār
package (parcel)	पार्सल (f)	pārsal
money transfer	मनी ट्रांसफर (m)	manī trānsafar

to receive (vt)	पाना	pāna
to send (vt)	भेजना	bhejana
sending	भेज (m)	bhej

address	पता (m)	pata
ZIP code	पिन कोड (m)	pin kod
sender	भेजनेवाला (m)	bhejanevāla
receiver	पानेवाला (m)	pānevāla

| name (first name) | पहला नाम (m) | pahala nām |
| surname (last name) | उपनाम (m) | upanām |

postage rate	डाक दर (m)	dāk dar
standard (adj)	मानक	mānak
economical (adj)	किफ़ायती	kifāyatī

| weight | वज़न (m) | vazan |
| to weigh (~ letters) | तोलना | tolana |

envelope	लिफ़ाफ़ा (m)	lifāfa
postage stamp	डाक टिकट (m)	dāk tikat
to stamp an envelope	डाक टिकट लगाना	dāk tikat lagāna

43. Banking

| bank | बैंक (m) | baink |
| branch (of bank, etc.) | शाखा (f) | shākha |

| bank clerk, consultant | क्लर्क (m) | klark |
| manager (director) | मैनेजर (m) | mainejar |

bank account	बैंक खाता (m)	baink khāta
account number	खाते का नम्बर (m)	khāte ka nambar
checking account	चालू खाता (m)	chālū khāta
savings account	बचत खाता (m)	bachat khāta

to open an account	खाता खोलना	khāta kholana
to close the account	खाता बंद करना	khāta band karana
to deposit into the account	खाते में जमा करना	khāte men jama karana
to withdraw (vt)	खाते से पैसा निकालना	khāte se paisa nikālana

| deposit | जमा (m) | jama |
| to make a deposit | जमा करना | jama karana |

| wire transfer | तार स्थानांतरण (m) | tār sthānāntaran |
| to wire, to transfer | पैसे स्थानांतरित करना | paise sthānāntarit karana |

| sum | रक़म (m) | raqam |
| How much? | कितना? | kitana? |

| signature | हस्ताक्षर (f) | hastākshar |
| to sign (vt) | हस्ताक्षर करना | hastākshar karana |

| credit card | क्रेडिट कार्ड (m) | kredit kārd |
| code (PIN code) | पिन कोड (m) | pin kod |

| credit card number | क्रेडिट कार्ड संख्या (f) | kredit kārd sankhya |
| ATM | एटीएम (m) | etīem |

check	चेक (m)	chek
to write a check	चेक लिखना	chek likhana
checkbook	चेकबुक (f)	chekabuk

loan (bank ~)	उधार (m)	uthār
to apply for a loan	उधार के लिए आवेदन करना	udhār ke lie āvedan karana
to get a loan	उधार लेना	uthār lena
to give a loan	उधार देना	uthār dena
guarantee	गारन्टी (f)	gārantī

44. Telephone. Phone conversation

telephone	फ़ोन (m)	fon
cell phone	मोबाइल फ़ोन (m)	mobail fon
answering machine	जवाबी मशीन (f)	javābī mashīn
to call (by phone)	फ़ोन करना	fon karana
phone call	कॉल (m)	kol
to dial a number	नम्बर लगाना	nambar lagāna
Hello!	हेलो!	helo!
to ask (vt)	पूछना	pūchhana
to answer (vi, vt)	जवाब देना	javāb dena
to hear (vt)	सुनना	sunana
well (adv)	ठीक	thīk
not well (adv)	ठीक नहीं	thīk nahin
noises (interference)	आवाज़ें (f)	āvāzen
receiver	रिसीवर (m)	risīvar
to pick up (~ the phone)	फ़ोन उठाना	fon uthāna
to hang up (~ the phone)	फ़ोन रखना	fon rakhana
busy (engaged)	बिज़ी	bizī
to ring (ab. phone)	फ़ोन बजना	fon bajana
telephone book	टेलीफ़ोन बुक (m)	telīfon buk
local (adj)	लोकल	lokal
long distance (~ call)	लंबी दूरी की कॉल	lambī dūrī kī kol
international (adj)	अंतरराष्ट्रीय	antarrāshtrīy

45. Cell phone

cell phone	मोबाइल फ़ोन (m)	mobail fon
display	डिस्प्ले (m)	disple
button	बटन (m)	batan
SIM card	सिम कार्ड (m)	sim kārd
battery	बैटरी (f)	baitarī
to be dead (battery)	बैटरी डेड हो जाना	baitarī ded ho jāna
charger	चार्जर (m)	chārjar
menu	मीनू (m)	mīnū
settings	सेटिंग्स (f)	setings
tune (melody)	कॉलर ट्यून (m)	kolar tyūn
to select (vt)	चुनना	chunana
calculator	कैल्कुलैटर (m)	kailkulaitar
voice mail	वॉयस मेल (f)	voyas mel
alarm clock	अलार्म घड़ी (f)	alārm gharī

contacts	संपर्क (m)	sampark
SMS (text message)	एसएसएमएस (m)	esemes
subscriber	सदस्य (m)	sadasy

46. Stationery

| ballpoint pen | बॉल पेन (m) | bol pen |
| fountain pen | फाउन्टेन पेन (m) | faunten pen |

pencil	पेंसिल (f)	pensil
highlighter	हाइलाइटर (m)	hailaitar
felt-tip pen	फ़ेल्ट टिप पेन (m)	felt tip pen

| notepad | नोटबुक (m) | notabuk |
| agenda (diary) | डायरी (f) | dāyarī |

ruler	स्केल (m)	skel
calculator	कैल्कुलेटर (m)	kailkuletar
eraser	रबड़ (f)	rabar
thumbtack	थंबटैक (m)	thanrbataik
paper clip	पेपर क्लिप (m)	pepar klip

glue	गोंद (f)	gond
stapler	स्टेप्लर (m)	steplar
hole punch	होल पंचर (m)	hol panchar
pencil sharpener	शार्पनर (m)	shārpanar

47. Foreign languages

language	भाषा (f)	bhāsha
foreign language	विदेशी भाषा (f)	videshī bhāsha
to study (vt)	पढ़ना	parhana
to learn (language, etc.)	सीखना	sīkhana

to read (vi, vt)	पढ़ना	parhana
to speak (vi, vt)	बोलना	bolana
to understand (vt)	समझना	samajhana
to write (vt)	लिखना	likhana

fast (adv)	तेज़	tez
slowly (adv)	धीरे	dhīre
fluently (adv)	धड़ल्ले से	dharalle se

rules	नियम (m pl)	niyam
grammar	व्याकरण (m)	vyākaran
vocabulary	शब्दावली (f)	shabdāvalī
phonetics	स्वरविज्ञान (m)	svaravigyān
textbook	पाठ्यपुस्तक (f)	pāthyapustak

dictionary	शब्दकोश (m)	shabdakosh
teach-yourself book	स्वयंशिक्षक पुस्तक (m)	svayanshikshak pustak
phrasebook	वार्तालाप-पुस्तिका (f)	vārttālāp-pustika
cassette, tape	कैसेट (f)	kaiset
videotape	वीडियो कैसेट (m)	vīdiyo kaiset
CD, compact disc	सीडी (m)	sīdī
DVD	डीवीडी (m)	dīvīdī
alphabet	वर्णमाला (f)	varnamāla
to spell (vt)	हिज्जे करना	hijje karana
pronunciation	उच्चारण (m)	uchchāran
accent	लहज़ा (m)	lahaza
with an accent	लहज़े के साथ	lahaze ke sāth
without an accent	बिना लहज़े	bina lahaze
word	शब्द (m)	shabd
meaning	मतलब (m)	matalab
course (e.g., a French ~)	पाठ्यक्रम (m)	pāthyakram
to sign up	सदस्य बनना	sadasy banana
teacher	शिक्षक (m)	shikshak
translation (process)	तर्जुमा (m)	tarjuma
translation (text, etc.)	अनुवाद (m)	anuvād
translator	अनुवादक (m)	anuvādak
interpreter	दुभाषिया (m)	dubhāshiya
polyglot	बहुभाषी (m)	bahubhāshī
memory	स्मृति (f)	smrti

MEALS. RESTAURANT

48. Table setting

spoon	चम्मच (m)	chammach
knife	छुरी (f)	chhurī
fork	काँटा (m)	kānta
cup (e.g., coffee ~)	प्याला (m)	pyāla
plate (dinner ~)	तश्तरी (f)	tashtarī
saucer	साॅसर (m)	sosar
napkin (on table)	नैपकीन (m)	naipakīn
toothpick	टूथपिक (m)	tūthapik

49. Restaurant

restaurant	रेस्टराँ (m)	restarān
coffee house	कॉफ़ी हाउस (m)	kofī haus
pub, bar	बार (m)	bār
tearoom	चायख़ाना (m)	chāyakhāna
waiter	बैरा (m)	baira
waitress	बैरी (f)	bairī
bartender	बारमैन (m)	bāramain
menu	मेनू (m)	menū
wine list	वाइन सूची (f)	vain sūchī
to book a table	मेज़ बुक करना	mez buk karana
course, dish	पकवान (m)	pakavān
to order (meal)	आर्डर देना	ārdar dena
to make an order	आर्डर देना	ārdar dena
aperitif	एपेरेतीफ़ (m)	eperetīf
appetizer	एपेटाइज़र (m)	epetaizar
dessert	मीठा (m)	mītha
check	बिल (m)	bil
to pay the check	बील का भुगतान करना	bīl ka bhugatān karana
to give change	खुले पैसे देना	khule paise dena
tip	टिप (f)	tip

50. Meals

food	खाना (m)	khāna
to eat (vi, vt)	खाना खाना	khāna khāna
breakfast	नाश्ता (m)	nāshta
to have breakfast	नाश्ता करना	nāshta karana
lunch	दोपहर का भोजन (m)	dopahar ka bhojan
to have lunch	दोपहर का भोजन करना	dopahar ka bhojan karana
dinner	रात्रिभोज (m)	rātribhoj
to have dinner	रात्रिभोज करना	rātribhoj karana
appetite	भूख (f)	bhūkh
Enjoy your meal!	अपने भोजन का आनंद उठाएं!	apane bhojan ka ānand uthaen!
to open (~ a bottle)	खोलना	kholana
to spill (liquid)	गिराना	girāna
to spill out (vi)	गिराना	girāna
to boil (vi)	उबालना	ubālana
to boil (vt)	उबालना	ubālana
boiled (~ water)	उबला हुआ	ubala hua
to chill, cool down (vt)	ठंडा करना	thanda karana
to chill (vi)	ठंडा करना	thanda karana
taste, flavor	स्वाद (m)	svād
aftertaste	स्वाद (m)	svād
to slim down (lose weight)	वज़न घटाना	vazan ghatāna
diet	डाइट (m)	dait
vitamin	विटामिन (m)	vitāmin
calorie	कैलोरी (f)	kailorī
vegetarian (n)	शाकाहारी (m)	shākāhārī
vegetarian (adj)	शाकाहारी	shākāhārī
fats (nutrient)	वसा (m pl)	vasa
proteins	प्रोटीन (m pl)	protīn
carbohydrates	कार्बोहाइड्रेट (m)	kārbohaidret
slice (of lemon, ham)	टुकड़ा (m)	tukara
piece (of cake, pie)	टुकड़ा (m)	tukara
crumb (of bread, cake, etc.)	टुकड़ा (m)	tukara

51. Cooked dishes

course, dish	पकवान (m)	pakavān
cuisine	व्यंजन (m)	vyanjan
recipe	रैसीपी (f)	raisīpī

portion	भाग (m)	bhāg
salad	सलाद (m)	salād
soup	सूप (m)	sūp

clear soup (broth)	यख़नी (f)	yakhanī
sandwich (bread)	सैन्डविच (m)	saindavich
fried eggs	आमलेट (m)	āmalet

| hamburger (beefburger) | हैमबर्गर (m) | haimabargar |
| beefsteak | बीफ़स्टीक (m) | bīfastīk |

side dish	साइड डिश (f)	said dish
spaghetti	स्पेघेटी (f)	speghetī
mashed potatoes	आलू भरता (f)	ālū bharata
pizza	पीट्ज़ा (f)	pītza
porridge (oatmeal, etc.)	दलिया (f)	daliya
omelet	आमलेट (m)	āmalet

boiled (e.g., ~ beef)	उबला	ubala
smoked (adj)	धुएँ में पकाया हुआ	dhuen men pakāya hua
fried (adj)	भुना	bhuna
dried (adj)	सूखा	sūkha
frozen (adj)	फ्रोज़न	frozan
pickled (adj)	अचार	achār

sweet (sugary)	मीठा	mītha
salty (adj)	नमकीन	namakīn
cold (adj)	ठंडा	thanda
hot (adj)	गरम	garam
bitter (adj)	कड़वा	karava
tasty (adj)	स्वादिष्ट	svādisht

to cook in boiling water	उबलते पानी में पकाना	ubalate pānī men pakāna
to cook (dinner)	खाना बनाना	khāna banāna
to fry (vt)	भूनना	bhūnana
to heat up (food)	गरम करना	garam karana

to salt (vt)	नमक डालना	namak dālana
to pepper (vt)	मिर्च डालना	mirch dālana
to grate (vt)	कद्दूकश करना	kaddūkash karana
peel (n)	छिलका (f)	chhilaka
to peel (vt)	छिलका निकलना	chhilaka nikalana

52. Food

meat	गोश्त (m)	gosht
chicken	चीकन (m)	chīkan
Rock Cornish hen (poussin)	रॉक कोर्निश मुर्गी (f)	rok kornish murgī
duck	बत्तख़ (f)	battakh

goose	हंस (m)	hans
game	शिकार के पशुपक्षी (f)	shikār ke pashupakshī
turkey	टर्की (m)	tarkī

pork	सुअर का गोश्त (m)	suar ka gosht
veal	बछड़े का गोश्त (m)	bachhare ka gosht
lamb	भेड़ का गोश्त (m)	bher ka gosht
beef	गाय का गोश्त (m)	gāy ka gosht
rabbit	खरगोश (m)	kharagosh

sausage (bologna, pepperoni, etc.)	सॉसेज (f)	sosej
vienna sausage (frankfurter)	वियना सॉसेज (m)	viyana sosej
bacon	बेकन (m)	bekan
ham	हैम (m)	haim
gammon	सुअर की जांघ (f)	suar kī jāngh

pâté	पिसा हुआ गोश्त (m)	pisa hua gosht
liver	जिगर (f)	jigar
hamburger (ground beef)	कीमा (m)	kīma
tongue	जीभ (m)	jībh

egg	अंडा (m)	anda
eggs	अंडे (m pl)	ande
egg white	अंडे की सफ़ेदी (m)	ande kī safedī
egg yolk	अंडे की ज़र्दी (m)	ande kī zardī

fish	मछली (f)	machhalī
seafood	समुद्री खाना (m)	samudrī khāna
caviar	मछली के अंडे (m)	machhalī ke ande

crab	केकड़ा (m)	kekara
shrimp	चिंगड़ा (m)	chingara
oyster	सीप (m)	sīp
spiny lobster	लोबस्टर (m)	lobastar
octopus	ओक्टोपस (m)	oktopas
squid	स्कीड (m)	skīd

sturgeon	स्टर्जन (f)	starjan
salmon	सालमन (m)	sālaman
halibut	हैलिबट (f)	hailibat

cod	कॉड (f)	kod
mackerel	माक्रैल (f)	mākrail
tuna	टूना (f)	tūna
eel	बाम मछली (f)	bām machhalī

trout	ट्राउट मछली (f)	traut machhalī
sardine	सार्डीन (f)	sārdīn
pike	पाइक (f)	paik
herring	हेरिंग मछली (f)	hering machhalī

bread	ब्रेड (f)	bred
cheese	पनीर (m)	panīr
sugar	चीनी (f)	chīnī
salt	नमक (m)	namak
rice	चावल (m)	chāval
pasta (macaroni)	पास्ता (m)	pāsta
noodles	नूडल्स (m)	nūdals
butter	मक्खन (m)	makkhan
vegetable oil	तेल (m)	tel
sunflower oil	सूरजमुखी तेल (m)	sūrajamukhī tel
margarine	नकली मक्खन (m)	nakalī makkhan
olives	जैतून (m)	jaitūn
olive oil	जैतून का तेल (m)	jaitūn ka tel
milk	दूध (m)	dūdh
condensed milk	रबड़ी (f)	rabarī
yogurt	दही (m)	dahī
sour cream	खट्टी क्रीम (f)	khattī krīm
cream (of milk)	मलाई (f pl)	malaī
mayonnaise	मेयोनेज़ (m)	meyonez
buttercream	क्रीम (m)	krīm
cereal grains (wheat, etc.)	अनाज के दाने (m)	anāj ke dāne
flour	आटा (m)	āta
canned food	डिब्बाबन्द खाना (m)	dibbāband khāna
cornflakes	कॉर्नफ्लेक्स (m)	kornafleks
honey	शहद (m)	shahad
jam	जैम (m)	jaim
chewing gum	चूइन्ग गाम (m)	chūing gam

53. Drinks

water	पानी (m)	pānī
drinking water	पीने का पानी (f)	pīne ka pānī
mineral water	मिनरल वॉटर (m)	minaral votar
still (adj)	स्टिल वॉटर	stil votar
carbonated (adj)	काबोनेटेड	kārboneted
sparkling (adj)	स्पार्कलिंग	spārkaling
ice	बर्फ़ (m)	barf
with ice	बर्फ़ के साथ	barf ke sāth
non-alcoholic (adj)	शराब रहित	sharāb rahit
soft drink	कोल्ड ड्रिंक (f)	kold drink
refreshing drink	शीतलक ड्रिंक (f)	shītalak drink

lemonade	लेमोनेड (m)	lemoned
liquors	शराब (m pl)	sharāb
wine	वाइन (f)	vain
white wine	सफ़ेद वाइन (f)	safed vain
red wine	लाल वाइन (f)	lāl vain

liqueur	लिकर (m)	likar
champagne	शैम्पेन (f)	shaimpen
vermouth	वर्मिठथ (f)	varmauth

whiskey	विस्की (f)	viskī
vodka	वोडका (m)	vodaka
gin	जिन (f)	jin
cognac	कोन्याक (m)	konyāk
rum	रम (m)	ram

coffee	कॉफ़ी (f)	kofī
black coffee	काली कॉफ़ी (f)	kālī kofī
coffee with milk	दूध के साथ कॉफ़ी (f)	dūdh ke sāth kofī
cappuccino	कैपूचिनो (f)	kaipūchino
instant coffee	इन्सटेन्ट-काफ़ी (f)	insatent-kāfī

milk	दूध (m)	dūdh
cocktail	कॉकटेल (m)	kokatel
milkshake	मिल्कशेक (m)	milkashek

juice	रस (m)	ras
tomato juice	टमाटर का रस (m)	tamātar ka ras
orange juice	संतरे का रस (m)	santare ka ras
freshly squeezed juice	ताज़ा रस (m)	tāza ras

beer	बियर (m)	biyar
light beer	हल्का बियर (m)	halka biyar
dark beer	डार्क बियर (m)	dārk biyar

tea	चाय (f)	chāy
black tea	काली चाय (f)	kālī chāy
green tea	हरी चाय (f)	harī chāy

54. Vegetables

| vegetables | सब्जियाँ (f pl) | sabziyān |
| greens | हरी सब्जियाँ (f) | harī sabziyān |

tomato	टमाटर (m)	tamātar
cucumber	खीरा (m)	khīra
carrot	गाजर (f)	gājar
potato	आलू (m)	ālū
onion	प्याज़ (m)	pyāz
garlic	लहसुन (m)	lahasun

cabbage	पत्ता गोभी (f)	patta gobhī
cauliflower	फूल गोभी (f)	fūl gobhī
Brussels sprouts	ब्रसेल्स स्प्राउट्स (m)	brasels sprauts
broccoli	ब्रोकोली (f)	brokolī
beetroot	चुकन्दर (m)	chukandar
eggplant	बैंगन (m)	baingan
zucchini	तुरई (f)	turī
pumpkin	कद्दू	kaddū
turnip	शलजम (f)	shalajam
parsley	अजमोद (f)	ajamod
dill	सोआ (m)	soa
lettuce	सलाद पत्ता (m)	salād patta
celery	सेलरी (m)	selarī
asparagus	एस्पैरेगस (m)	espairegas
spinach	पालक (m)	pālak
pea	मटर (m)	matar
beans	फली (f pl)	falī
corn (maize)	मकई (f)	makī
kidney bean	राजमा (f)	rājama
bell pepper	शिमला मिर्च (m)	shimala mirch
radish	मूली (f)	mūlī
artichoke	हाथीचक (m)	hāthīchak

55. Fruits. Nuts

fruit	फल (m)	fal
apple	सेब (m)	seb
pear	नाशपाती (f)	nāshapātī
lemon	नींबू (m)	nīmbū
orange	संतरा (m)	santara
strawberry (garden ~)	स्ट्रॉबेरी (f)	stroberī
mandarin	नारंगी (m)	nārangī
plum	आलूबुखारा (m)	ālūbukhāra
peach	आड़ू (m)	ārū
apricot	खूबानी (f)	khūbānī
raspberry	रसभरी (f)	rasabharī
pineapple	अनानास (m)	anānās
banana	केला (m)	kela
watermelon	तरबूज (m)	tarabūz
grape	अंगूर (m)	angūr
cherry	चेरी (f)	cherī
melon	खरबूजा (f)	kharabūza
grapefruit	ग्रेपफ्रूट (m)	grepafrūt
avocado	एवोकाडो (m)	evokādo

papaya	पपीता (f)	papīta
mango	आम (m)	ām
pomegranate	अनार (m)	anār

redcurrant	लाल किशमिश (f)	lāl kishamish
blackcurrant	काली किशमिश (f)	kālī kishamish
gooseberry	आमला (f)	āmala
bilberry	बिलबेरी (f)	bilaberī
blackberry	ब्लैकबेरी (f)	blaikaberī

raisin	किशमिश (m)	kishamish
fig	अंजीर (m)	anjīr
date	खजूर (m)	khajūr

peanut	मूँगफली (m)	mūngafalī
almond	बादाम (f)	bādām
walnut	अखरोट (m)	akharot
hazelnut	हेज़लनट (m)	hezalanat
coconut	नारियल (m)	nāriyal
pistachios	पिस्ता (m)	pista

56. Bread. Candy

bakers' confectionery (pastry)	मिठाई (f pl)	mithaī
bread	ब्रेड (f)	bred
cookies	बिस्कुट (m)	biskut

chocolate (n)	चॉकलेट (m)	chokalet
chocolate (as adj)	चॉकलेटी	chokaletī
candy (wrapped)	टॉफ़ी (f)	tofī
cake (e.g., cupcake)	पेस्ट्री (f)	pestrī
cake (e.g., birthday ~)	केक (m)	kek

| pie (e.g., apple ~) | पाई (m) | paī |
| filling (for cake, pie) | फ़िलिंग (f) | filing |

jam (whole fruit jam)	जैम (m)	jaim
marmalade	मुरब्बा (m)	murabba
waffles	वेफ़र (m pl)	vefar
ice-cream	आईस-क्रीम (f)	āīs-krīm

57. Spices

salt	नमक (m)	namak
salty (adj)	नमकीन	namakīn
to salt (vt)	नमक डालना	namak dālana
black pepper	काली मिर्च (f)	kālī mirch

red pepper (milled ~)	लाल मिर्च (m)	lāl mirch
mustard	सरसों (m)	sarason
horseradish	अरब मूली (f)	arab mūlī
condiment	मसाला (m)	masāla
spice	मसाला (m)	masāla
sauce	चटनी (f)	chatanī
vinegar	सिरका (m)	siraka
anise	सौंफ़ (f)	saumf
basil	तुलसी (f)	tulasī
cloves	लौंग (f)	laung
ginger	अदरक (m)	adarak
coriander	धनिया (m)	dhaniya
cinnamon	दालचीनी (f)	dālachīnī
sesame	तिल (m)	til
bay leaf	तेजपत्ता (m)	tejapatta
paprika	लाल शिमला मिर्च पाउडर (m)	lāl shimala mirch paudar
caraway	ज़ीरा (m)	zīra
saffron	ज़ाफ़रान (m)	zāfarān

PERSONAL INFORMATION. FAMILY

58. Personal information. Forms

name (first name)	पहला नाम (m)	pahala nām
surname (last name)	उपनाम (m)	upanām
date of birth	जन्म-दिवस (m)	janm-divas
place of birth	मातृभूमि (f)	mātrbhūmi
nationality	नागरिकता (f)	nāgarikata
place of residence	निवास स्थान (m)	nivās sthān
country	देश (m)	desh
profession (occupation)	पेशा (m)	pesha
gender, sex	लिंग (m)	ling
height	क़द (m)	qad
weight	वज़न (m)	vazan

59. Family members. Relatives

mother	माँ (f)	mān
father	पिता (m)	pita
son	बेटा (m)	beta
daughter	बेटी (f)	betī
younger daughter	छोटी बेटी (f)	chhotī betī
younger son	छोटा बेटा (m)	chhota beta
eldest daughter	बड़ी बेटी (f)	barī betī
eldest son	बड़ा बेटा (m)	bara beta
brother	भाई (m)	bhaī
sister	बहन (f)	bahan
cousin (masc.)	चचेरा भाई (m)	chachera bhaī
cousin (fem.)	चचेरी बहन (f)	chacherī bahan
mom, mommy	अम्मा (f)	amma
dad, daddy	पापा (m)	pāpa
parents	माँ-बाप (m pl)	mān-bāp
child	बच्चा (m)	bachcha
children	बच्चे (m pl)	bachche
grandmother	दादी (f)	dādī
grandfather	दादा (m)	dāda
grandson	पोता (m)	pota

granddaughter	पोती (f)	potī
grandchildren	पोते (m)	pote
uncle	चाचा (m)	chācha
aunt	चाची (f)	chāchī
nephew	भतीजा (m)	bhatīja
niece	भतीजी (f)	bhatījī
mother-in-law (wife's mother)	सास (f)	sās
father-in-law (husband's father)	ससुर (m)	sasur
son-in-law (daughter's husband)	दामाद (m)	dāmād
stepmother	सौतेली माँ (f)	sautelī mān
stepfather	सौतेले पिता (m)	sautele pita
infant	दूधमुँहा बच्चा (m)	dudhamunha bachcha
baby (infant)	शिशु (f)	shishu
little boy, kid	छोटा बच्चा (m)	chhota bachcha
wife	पत्नी (f)	patnī
husband	पति (m)	pati
spouse (husband)	पति (m)	pati
spouse (wife)	पत्नी (f)	patnī
married (masc.)	शादीशुदा	shādīshuda
married (fem.)	शादीशुदा	shādīshuda
single (unmarried)	अविवाहित	avivāhit
bachelor	कुँआरा (m)	kunāra
divorced (masc.)	तलाक़शुदा	talāqashuda
widow	विधवा (f)	vidhava
widower	विधुर (m)	vidhur
relative	रिश्तेदार (m)	rishtedār
close relative	सम्बंधी (m)	sambandhī
distant relative	दूर का रिश्तेदार (m)	dūr ka rishtedār
relatives	रिश्तेदार (m pl)	rishtedār
orphan (boy or girl)	अनाथ (m)	anāth
guardian (of a minor)	अभिभावक (m)	abhibhāvak
to adopt (a boy)	लड़का गोद लेना	laraka god lena
to adopt (a girl)	लड़की गोद लेना	larakī god lena

60. Friends. Coworkers

friend (masc.)	दोस्त (m)	dost
friend (fem.)	सहेली (f)	sahelī
friendship	दोस्ती (f)	dostī
to be friends	दोस्त होना	dost hona

buddy (masc.)	मित्र (m)	mitr
buddy (fem.)	सहेली (f)	sahelī
partner	पार्टनर (m)	pārtanar
chief (boss)	चीफ़ (m)	chīf
superior (n)	अधीक्षक (m)	adhīkshak
subordinate (n)	अधीनस्थ (m)	adhīnasth
colleague	सहकर्मी (m)	sahakarmī
acquaintance (person)	परिचित आदमी (m)	parichit ādamī
fellow traveler	सहगामी (m)	sahagāmī
classmate	सहपाठी (m)	sahapāthī
neighbor (masc.)	पड़ोसी (m)	parosī
neighbor (fem.)	पड़ोसन (f)	parosan
neighbors	पड़ोसी (m pl)	parosī

HUMAN BODY. MEDICINE

61. Head

head	सिर (m)	sir
face	चेहरा (m)	chehara
nose	नाक (f)	nāk
mouth	मुँह (m)	munh
eye	आँख (f)	ānkh
eyes	आँखें (f)	ānkhen
pupil	आँख की पुतली (f)	ānkh kī putalī
eyebrow	भौंह (f)	bhaunh
eyelash	बरौनी (f)	baraunī
eyelid	पलक (m)	palak
tongue	जीभ (m)	jībh
tooth	दाँत (f)	dānt
lips	होंठ (m)	honth
cheekbones	गाल की हड्डी (f)	gāl kī haddī
gum	मसूड़ा (m)	masūra
palate	तालु (m)	tālu
nostrils	नथने (m pl)	nathane
chin	ठोड़ी (f)	thorī
jaw	जबड़ा (m)	jabara
cheek	गाल (m)	gāl
forehead	माथा (m)	mātha
temple	कनपट्टी (f)	kanapattī
ear	कान (m)	kān
back of the head	सिर का पिछला हिस्सा (m)	sir ka pichhala hissa
neck	गरदन (m)	garadan
throat	गला (m)	gala
hair	बाल (m pl)	bāl
hairstyle	हेयरस्टाइल (m)	heyarastail
haircut	हेयरकट (m)	heyarakat
wig	नकली बाल (m)	nakalī bāl
mustache	मूँछें (f pl)	mūnchhen
beard	दाढ़ी (f)	dārhī
to have (a beard, etc.)	होना	hona
braid	चोटी (f)	chotī
sideburns	गलमुच्छा (m)	galamuchchha
red-haired (adj)	लाल बाल	lāl bāl

gray (hair)	सफ़ेद बाल	safed bāl
bald (adj)	गंजा	ganja
bald patch	गंजाई (f)	ganjaī
ponytail	पोनी-टेल (f)	ponī-tel
bangs	बेंग (m)	beng

62. Human body

hand	हाथ (m)	hāth
arm	बाँह (m)	bānh
finger	उँगली (m)	ungalī
thumb	अँगूठा (m)	angūtha
little finger	छोटी उंगली (f)	chhotī ungalī
nail	नाख़ून (m)	nākhūn
fist	मुट्ठी (m)	mutthī
palm	हथेली (f)	hathelī
wrist	कलाई (f)	kalaī
forearm	प्रकोष्ठ (m)	prakoshth
elbow	कोहनी (f)	kohanī
shoulder	कंधा (m)	kandha
leg	टाँग (f)	tāng
foot	पैर का तलवा (m)	pair ka talava
knee	घुटना (m)	ghutana
calf (part of leg)	पिंडली (f)	pindalī
hip	जाँघ (f)	jāngh
heel	एड़ी (f)	erī
body	शरीर (m)	sharīr
stomach	पेट (m)	pet
chest	सीना (m)	sīna
breast	स्तन (f)	stan
flank	कूल्हा (m)	kūlha
back	पीठ (f)	pīth
lower back	पीठ का निचला हिस्सा (m)	pīth ka nichala hissa
waist	कमर (f)	kamar
navel (belly button)	नाभी (f)	nābhī
buttocks	नितंब (m pl)	nitamb
bottom	नितम्ब (m)	nitamb
beauty mark	सौंदर्य चिन्ह (f)	saundary chinh
birthmark	जन्म चिह्न (m)	janm chihn
(café au lait spot)		
tattoo	टैटू (m)	taitū
scar	घाव का निशान (m)	ghāv ka nishān

63. Diseases

sickness	बीमारी (f)	bīmārī
to be sick	बीमार होना	bīmār hona
health	सेहत (f)	sehat
runny nose (coryza)	नज़ला (m)	nazala
tonsillitis	टॉन्सिल (m)	tonsil
cold (illness)	जुकाम (f)	zukām
to catch a cold	जुकाम हो जाना	zukām ho jāna
bronchitis	ब्रॉन्काइटिस (m)	bronkaitis
pneumonia	निमोनिया (f)	nimoniya
flu, influenza	फ्लू (m)	flū
nearsighted (adj)	कमबीन	kamabīn
farsighted (adj)	कमज़ोर दूरदृष्टि	kamazor dūradrshti
strabismus (crossed eyes)	तिरछी नज़र (m)	tirachhī nazar
cross-eyed (adj)	तिरछी नज़रवाला	tirachhī nazaravāla
cataract	मोतिया बिंद (m)	motiya bind
glaucoma	काला मोतिया (m)	kāla motiya
stroke	स्ट्रोक (m)	strok
heart attack	दिल का दौरा (m)	dil ka daura
myocardial infarction	मायोकार्डियल इन्फ्राक्शन (m)	māyokārdiyal infārkshan
paralysis	लकवा (m)	lakava
to paralyze (vt)	लक़वा मारना	laqava mārana
allergy	एलर्जी (f)	elarjī
asthma	दमा (f)	dama
diabetes	शूगर (f)	shūgar
toothache	दाँत दर्द (m)	dānt dard
caries	दाँत में कीड़ा (m)	dānt men kīra
diarrhea	दस्त (m)	dast
constipation	कब्ज़ (m)	kabz
stomach upset	पेट ख़राब (m)	pet kharāb
food poisoning	ख़राब खाने से हुई बीमारी (f)	kharāb khāne se huī bīmārī
to get food poisoning	ख़राब खाने से बीमार पड़ना	kharāb khāne se bīmar parana
arthritis	गठिया (m)	gathiya
rickets	बालवक्र (m)	bālavakr
rheumatism	आमवात (m)	āmavāt
atherosclerosis	धमनीकलाकाठिन्य (m)	dhamanīkalākāthiny
gastritis	जठर-शोथ (m)	jathar-shoth
appendicitis	उण्डुक-शोथ (m)	unduk-shoth

| cholecystitis | पित्ताशय (m) | pittāshay |
| ulcer | अल्सर (m) | alsar |

measles	मीज़ल्स (m)	mīzals
rubella (German measles)	जर्मन मीज़ल्स (m)	jarman mīzals
jaundice	पीलिया (m)	pīliya
hepatitis	हेपेटाइटिस (m)	hepetaitis

schizophrenia	शीज़ोफ्रेनीय (f)	shīzofrenīy
rabies (hydrophobia)	रेबीज़ (m)	rebīz
neurosis	न्यूरोसिस (m)	nyūrosis
concussion	आघात (m)	āghāt

cancer	कर्क रोग (m)	kark rog
sclerosis	काठिन्य (m)	kāthiny
multiple sclerosis	मल्टीपल स्क्लेरोसिस (m)	maltīpal sklerosis

alcoholism	शराबीपन (m)	sharābīpan
alcoholic (n)	शराबी (m)	sharābī
syphilis	सीफ़िलिस (m)	sīfīlis
AIDS	ऐड्स (m)	aids

tumor	ट्यूमर (m)	tyūmar
malignant (adj)	घातक	ghātak
benign (adj)	अर्बुद	arbud

fever	बुखार (m)	bukhār
malaria	मलेरिया (f)	maleriya
gangrene	गैन्ग्रीन (m)	gaingrīn
seasickness	जहाज़ी मतली (f)	jahāzī matalī
epilepsy	मिरगी (f)	miragī

epidemic	महामारी (f)	mahāmārī
typhus	टाइफ़स (m)	taifas
tuberculosis	टीबी (m)	tībī
cholera	हैज़ा (f)	haiza
plague (bubonic ~)	प्लेग (f)	pleg

64. Symptoms. Treatments. Part 1

symptom	लक्षण (m)	lakshan
temperature	तापमान (m)	tāpamān
high temperature (fever)	बुखार (f)	bukhār
pulse	नब्ज़ (f)	nabz

dizziness (vertigo)	सिर का चक्कर (m)	sir ka chakkar
hot (adj)	गरम	garam
shivering	कंपकंपी (f)	kampakampī
pale (e.g., ~ face)	पीला	pīla
cough	खाँसी (f)	khānsī

to cough (vi)	खाँसना	khānsana
to sneeze (vi)	छींकना	chhīnkana
faint	बेहोशी (f)	behoshī
to faint (vi)	बेहोश होना	behosh hona
bruise (hématome)	नील (m)	nīl
bump (lump)	गुमड़ा (m)	gumara
to bang (bump)	चोट लगना	chot lagana
contusion (bruise)	चोट (f)	chot
to get a bruise	घाव लगना	ghāv lagana
to limp (vi)	लँगड़ाना	langarāna
dislocation	हड्डी खिसकना (f)	haddī khisakana
to dislocate (vt)	हड्डी खिसकना	haddī khisakana
fracture	हड्डी टूट जाना (f)	haddī tūt jāna
to have a fracture	हड्डी टूट जाना	haddī tūt jāna
cut (e.g., paper ~)	कट जाना (m)	kat jāna
to cut oneself	ख़ुद को काट लेना	khud ko kāt lena
bleeding	रक्त-स्राव (m)	rakt-srāv
burn (injury)	जला होना	jala hona
to get burned	जल जाना	jal jāna
to prick (vt)	चुभाना	chubhāna
to prick oneself	ख़ुद को चुभाना	khud ko chubhāna
to injure (vt)	घायल करना	ghāyal karana
injury	चोट (f)	chot
wound	घाव (m)	ghāv
trauma	चोट (f)	chot
to be delirious	बेहोशी में बड़बड़ाना	behoshī men barabadāna
to stutter (vi)	हकलाना	hakalāna
sunstroke	धूप आघात (m)	dhūp āghāt

65. Symptoms. Treatments. Part 2

pain, ache	दर्द (f)	dard
splinter (in foot, etc.)	चुभ जाना (m)	chubh jāna
sweat (perspiration)	पसीना (f)	pasīna
to sweat (perspire)	पसीना निकलना	pasīna nikalana
vomiting	वमन (m)	vaman
convulsions	दौरा (m)	daura
pregnant (adj)	गर्भवती	garbhavatī
to be born	जन्म लेना	janm lena
delivery, labor	पैदा करना (m)	paida karana
to deliver (~ a baby)	पैदा करना	paida karana
abortion	गर्भपात (m)	garbhapāt

breathing, respiration	साँस (f)	sāns
in-breath (inhalation)	साँस अंदर खींचना (f)	sāns andar khīnchana
out-breath (exhalation)	साँस बाहर छोड़ना (f)	sāns bāhar chhorana
to exhale (breathe out)	साँस बाहर छोड़ना	sāns bāhar chhorana
to inhale (vi)	साँस अंदर खींचना	sāns andar khīnchana

disabled person	अपाहिज (m)	apāhij
cripple	लूला (m)	lūla
drug addict	नशेबाज़ (m)	nashebāz

deaf (adj)	बहरा	bahara
mute (adj)	गूँगा	gūnga
deaf mute (adj)	बहरा और गूँगा	bahara aur gūnga

mad, insane (adj)	पागल	pāgal
madman (demented person)	पगला (m)	pagala
madwoman	पगली (f)	pagalī
to go insane	पागल हो जाना	pāgal ho jāna

gene	वंशाणु (m)	vanshānu
immunity	रोग प्रतिरोधक शक्ति (f)	rog pratirodhak shakti
hereditary (adj)	जन्मजात	janmajāt
congenital (adj)	पैदाइशी	paidaishī

virus	विषाणु (m)	vishānu
microbe	कीटाणु (m)	kītānu
bacterium	जीवाणु (m)	jīvānu
infection	संक्रमण (m)	sankraman

66. Symptoms. Treatments. Part 3

| hospital | अस्पताल (m) | aspatāl |
| patient | मरीज़ (m) | marīz |

diagnosis	रोग-निर्णय (m)	rog-nirnay
cure	इलाज (m)	ilāj
medical treatment	चिकित्सीय उपचार (m)	chikitsīy upachār
to get treatment	इलाज कराना	ilāj karāna
to treat (~ a patient)	इलाज करना	ilāj karana
to nurse (look after)	देखभाल करना	dekhabhāl karana
care (nursing ~)	देखभाल (f)	dekhabhāl

operation, surgery	ऑपरेशन (m)	opareshan
to bandage (head, limb)	पट्टी बाँधना	pattī bāndhana
bandaging	पट्टी (f)	pattī

vaccination	टीका (m)	tīka
to vaccinate (vt)	टीका लगाना	tīka lagāna
injection, shot	इंजेक्शन (m)	injekshan

to give an injection	इंजेक्शन लगाना	injekshan lagāna
amputation	अंगविच्छेद (f)	angavichchhed
to amputate (vt)	अंगविच्छेद करना	angavichchhed karana
coma	कोमा (m)	koma
to be in a coma	कोमा में चले जाना	koma men chale jāna
intensive care	गहन चिकित्सा (f)	gahan chikitsa
to recover (~ from flu)	ठीक हो जाना	thīk ho jāna
condition (patient's ~)	हालत (m)	hālat
consciousness	होश (m)	hosh
memory (faculty)	याददाश्त (f)	yādadāsht
to pull out (tooth)	दाँत निकालना	dānt nikālana
filling	भराव (m)	bharāv
to fill (a tooth)	दाँत को भरना	dānt ko bharana
hypnosis	हिपनोसिस (m)	hipanosis
to hypnotize (vt)	हिपनोटाइज़ करना	hipanotaiz karana

67. Medicine. Drugs. Accessories

medicine, drug	दवा (f)	dava
remedy	दवाई (f)	davaī
to prescribe (vt)	नुसख़ा लिखना	nusakha likhana
prescription	नुसख़ा (m)	nusakha
tablet, pill	गोली (f)	golī
ointment	मरहम (m)	maraham
ampule	एम्प्यूल (m)	empyūl
mixture	सिरप (m)	sirap
syrup	शरबत (m)	sharabat
pill	गोली (f)	golī
powder	चूरन (m)	chūran
gauze bandage	पट्टी (f)	pattī
cotton wool	रूई का गोला (m)	rūī ka gola
iodine	आयोडीन (m)	āyodīn
Band-Aid	बैंड-एड (m)	baind-ed
eyedropper	आई-ड्रॉपर (m)	āī-dropar
thermometer	थरमामीटर (m)	tharamāmītar
syringe	इंजेक्शन (m)	injekshan
wheelchair	व्हीलचेयर (f)	vhīlacheyar
crutches	बैसाखी (m pl)	baisākhī
painkiller	दर्द-निवारक (f)	dard-nivārak
laxative	जुलाब की गोली (f)	julāb kī golī
spirits (ethanol)	स्पिरिट (m)	spirit
medicinal herbs	जड़ी-बूटी (f)	jarī-būtī
herbal (~ tea)	जड़ी-बूटियों से बना	jarī-būtiyon se bana

APARTMENT

68. Apartment

apartment	प्रलैट (f)	flait
room	कमरा (m)	kamara
bedroom	सोने का कमरा (m)	sone ka kamara
dining room	खाने का कमरा (m)	khāne ka kamara
living room	बैठक (f)	baithak
study (home office)	घरेलू कार्यालय (m)	gharelū kāryālay
entry room	प्रवेश कक्ष (m)	pravesh kaksh
bathroom (room with a bath or shower)	स्नानघर (m)	snānaghar
half bath	शौचालय (m)	shauchālay
ceiling	छत (f)	chhat
floor	फ़र्श (m)	farsh
corner	कोना (m)	kona

69. Furniture. Interior

furniture	फ़र्निचर (m)	farnichar
table	मेज़ (f)	mez
chair	कुर्सी (f)	kursī
bed	पलंग (m)	palang
couch, sofa	सोफ़ा (m)	sofa
armchair	हत्थे वाली कुर्सी (f)	hatthe vālī kursī
bookcase	किताबों की अलमारी (f)	kitābon kī alamārī
shelf	शेल्फ़ (f)	shelf
wardrobe	कपड़ों की अलमारी (f)	kaparon kī alamārī
coat rack (wall-mounted ~)	खूँटी (f)	khūntī
coat stand	खूँटी (f)	khūntī
bureau, dresser	कपड़ों की अलमारी (f)	kaparon kī alamārī
coffee table	कॉफ़ी की मेज़ (f)	kofī kī mez
mirror	आईना (m)	āīna
carpet	कालीन (m)	kālīn
rug, small carpet	दरी (f)	darī
fireplace	चिमनी (f)	chimanī
candle	मोमबत्ती (f)	momabattī

candlestick	मोमबत्तीदान (m)	momabattīdān
drapes	परदे (m pl)	parade
wallpaper	वॉल पेपर (m)	vol pepar
blinds (jalousie)	जेलुज़ी (f pl)	jeluzī
table lamp	मेज़ का लैम्प (m)	mez ka laimp
wall lamp (sconce)	दिवार का लैम्प (m)	divār ka laimp
floor lamp	फ़र्श का लैम्प (m)	farsh ka laimp
chandelier	झूमर (m)	jhūmar
leg (of chair, table)	पाँव (m)	pānv
armrest	कुर्सी का हत्था (m)	kursī ka hattha
back (backrest)	कुर्सी की पीठ (f)	kursī kī pīth
drawer	दराज़ (m)	darāz

70. Bedding

bedclothes	बिस्तर के कपड़े (m)	bistar ke kapare
pillow	तकिया (m)	takiya
pillowcase	ग़िलाफ़ (m)	gilāf
duvet, comforter	रज़ाई (f)	razaī
sheet	चादर (f)	chādar
bedspread	चादर (f)	chādar

71. Kitchen

kitchen	रसोईघर (m)	rasoīghar
gas	गैस (m)	gais
gas stove (range)	गैस का चूल्हा (m)	gais ka chūlha
electric stove	बिजली का चूल्हा (m)	bijalī ka chūlha
oven	ओवन (m)	ovan
microwave oven	माइक्रोवेव ओवन (m)	maikrovev ovan
refrigerator	फ़्रिज (m)	frij
freezer	फ़्रीजर (m)	frījar
dishwasher	डिशवॉशर (m)	dishavoshar
meat grinder	कीमा बनाने की मशीन (f)	kīma banāne kī mashīn
juicer	जूसर (m)	jūsar
toaster	टोस्टर (m)	tostar
mixer	मिक्सर (m)	miksar
coffee machine	कॉफ़ी मशीन (f)	kofī mashīn
coffee pot	कॉफ़ी पॉट (m)	kofī pot
coffee grinder	कॉफ़ी पीसने की मशीन (f)	kofī pīsane kī mashīn
kettle	केतली (f)	ketalī
teapot	चायदानी (f)	chāyadānī

lid	ढक्कन (m)	dhakkan
tea strainer	छलनी (f)	chhalanī
spoon	चम्मच (m)	chammach
teaspoon	चम्मच (m)	chammach
soup spoon	चम्मच (m)	chammach
fork	काँटा (m)	kānta
knife	छुरी (f)	chhurī
tableware (dishes)	बरतन (m)	baratan
plate (dinner ~)	तश्तरी (f)	tashtarī
saucer	तश्तरी (f)	tashtarī
shot glass	जाम (m)	jām
glass (tumbler)	गिलास (m)	gilās
cup	प्याला (m)	pyāla
sugar bowl	चीनीदानी (f)	chīnīdānī
salt shaker	नमकदानी (m)	namakadānī
pepper shaker	मिर्चदानी (f)	mirchadānī
butter dish	मक्खनदानी (f)	makkhanadānī
stock pot (soup pot)	सॉसपैन (m)	sosapain
frying pan (skillet)	फ़्राइ पैन (f)	frai pain
ladle	डोई (f)	doī
colander	कालेन्डर (m)	kālendar
tray (serving ~)	थाली (m)	thālī
bottle	बोतल (f)	botal
jar (glass)	शीशी (f)	shīshī
can	डिब्बा (m)	dibba
bottle opener	बोतल ओपनर (m)	botal opanar
can opener	ओपनर (m)	opanar
corkscrew	पेंचकस (m)	penchakas
filter	फ़िल्टर (m)	filtar
to filter (vt)	फ़िल्टर करना	filtar karana
trash, garbage (food waste, etc.)	कूड़ा (m)	kūra
trash can (kitchen ~)	कूड़े की बाल्टी (f)	kūre kī bāltī

72. Bathroom

bathroom	स्नानघर (m)	snānaghar
water	पानी (m)	pānī
faucet	नल (m)	nal
hot water	गरम पानी (m)	garam pānī
cold water	ठंडा पानी (m)	thanda pānī
toothpaste	टूथपेस्ट (m)	tūthapest

to brush one's teeth	दाँत ब्रश करना	dānt brash karana
to shave (vi)	शेव करना	shev karana
shaving foam	शेविंग फ़ोम (m)	sheving fom
razor	रेज़र (f)	rezar
to wash (one's hands, etc.)	धोना	dhona
to take a bath	नहाना	nahāna
shower	शावर (m)	shāvar
to take a shower	शावर लेना	shāvar lena
bathtub	बाथटब (m)	bāthatab
toilet (toilet bowl)	संडास (m)	sandās
sink (washbasin)	सिंक (m)	sink
soap	साबुन (m)	sābun
soap dish	साबुनदानी (f)	sābunadānī
sponge	स्पंज (f)	spanj
shampoo	शैम्पू (m)	shaimpū
towel	तौलिया (f)	tauliya
bathrobe	चोगा (m)	choga
laundry (process)	धुलाई (f)	dhulaī
washing machine	वॉशिंग मशीन (f)	voshing mashīn
to do the laundry	कपड़े धोना	kapare dhona
laundry detergent	कपड़े धोने का पाउडर (m)	kapare dhone ka paudar

73. Household appliances

TV set	टीवी सेट (m)	tīvī set
tape recorder	टेप रिकार्डर (m)	tep rikārdar
VCR (video recorder)	वीडियो टेप रिकार्डर (m)	vīdiyo tep rikārdar
radio	रेडियो (m)	rediyo
player (CD, MP3, etc.)	प्लेयर (m)	pleyar
video projector	वीडियो प्रोजेक्टर (m)	vīdiyo projektar
home movie theater	होम थीएटर (m)	hom thīetar
DVD player	डीवीडी प्लेयर (m)	dīvīdī pleyar
amplifier	ध्वनि-विस्तारक (m)	dhvani-vistārak
video game console	वीडियो गेम कन्सोल (m)	vīdiyo gem kansol
video camera	वीडियो कैमरा (m)	vīdiyo kaimara
camera (photo)	कैमरा (m)	kaimara
digital camera	डीजिटल कैमरा (m)	dījital kaimara
vacuum cleaner	वैक्यूम क्लीनर (m)	vaikyūm klīnar
iron (e.g., steam ~)	इस्तरी (f)	istarī
ironing board	इस्तरी तख़्ता (m)	istarī takhta
telephone	टेलीफ़ोन (m)	telīfon
cell phone	मोबाइल फ़ोन (m)	mobail fon

| typewriter | टाइपराइटर (m) | taiparaitar |
| sewing machine | सिलाई मशीन (f) | silaī mashīn |

microphone	माइक्रोफ़ोन (m)	maikrofon
headphones	हैड्फ़ोन (m pl)	hairafon
remote control (TV)	रिमोट (m)	rimot

CD, compact disc	सीडी (m)	sīdī
cassette, tape	कैसेट (f)	kaiset
vinyl record	रिकार्ड (m)	rikārd

THE EARTH. WEATHER

74. Outer space

space	अंतरिक्ष (m)	antariksh
space (as adj)	अंतरिक्षीय	antarikshīy
outer space	अंतरिक्ष (m)	antariksh
universe	ब्रह्माण्ड (m)	brahmānd
galaxy	आकाशगंगा (f)	ākāshaganga
star	सितारा (m)	sitāra
constellation	नक्षत्र (m)	nakshatr
planet	ग्रह (m)	grah
satellite	उपग्रह (m)	upagrah
meteorite	उल्का पिंड (m)	ulka pind
comet	पुच्छल तारा (m)	puchchhal tāra
asteroid	ग्रहिका (f)	grahika
orbit	ग्रहपथ (m)	grahapath
to revolve (~ around the Earth)	चक्कर लगना	chakkar lagana
atmosphere	वातावरण (m)	vātāvaran
the Sun	सूरज (m)	sūraj
solar system	सौर प्रणाली (f)	saur pranālī
solar eclipse	सूर्य ग्रहण (m)	sūry grahan
the Earth	पृथ्वी (f)	prthvī
the Moon	चाँद (m)	chānd
Mars	मंगल (m)	mangal
Venus	शुक्र (m)	shukr
Jupiter	बृहस्पति (m)	brhaspati
Saturn	शनि (m)	shani
Mercury	बुध (m)	budh
Uranus	अरुण (m)	arun
Neptune	वरुण (m)	varūn
Pluto	प्लूटो (m)	plūto
Milky Way	आकाश गंगा (f)	ākāsh ganga
Great Bear (Ursa Major)	सप्तर्षिमंडल (m)	saptarshimandal
North Star	ध्रुव तारा (m)	dhruv tāra
Martian	मंगल ग्रह का निवासी (m)	mangal grah ka nivāsī
extraterrestrial (n)	अन्य नक्षत्र का निवासी (m)	any nakshatr ka nivāsī

alien	अन्य नक्षत्र का निवासी (m)	any nakshatr ka nivāsī
flying saucer	उड़न तश्तरी (f)	uran tashtarī
spaceship	अंतरिक्ष विमान (m)	antariksh vimān
space station	अंतरिक्ष अड्डा (m)	antariksh adda
blast-off	चालू करना (m)	chālū karana
engine	इंजन (m)	injan
nozzle	नोज़ल (m)	nozal
fuel	ईंधन (m)	īndhan
cockpit, flight deck	केबिन (m)	kebin
antenna	एरियल (m)	eriyal
porthole	विमान गवाक्ष (m)	vimān gavāksh
solar panel	सौर पेनल (m)	saur penal
spacesuit	अंतरिक्ष पोशाक (m)	antariksh poshāk
weightlessness	भारहीनता (m)	bhārahīnata
oxygen	आक्सीजन (m)	āksījan
docking (in space)	डॉकिंग (f)	doking
to dock (vi, vt)	डॉकिंग करना	doking karana
observatory	वेधशाला (m)	vedhashāla
telescope	दूरबीन (f)	dūrabīn
to observe (vt)	देखना	dekhana
to explore (vt)	जाँचना	jānchana

75. The Earth

the Earth	पृथ्वी (f)	prthvī
the globe (the Earth)	गोला (m)	gola
planet	ग्रह (m)	grah
atmosphere	वातावरण (m)	vātāvaran
geography	भूगोल (m)	bhūgol
nature	प्रकृति (f)	prakrti
globe (table ~)	गोलक (m)	golak
map	नक्शा (m)	naksha
atlas	मानचित्रावली (f)	mānachitrāvalī
Europe	यूरोप (m)	yūrop
Asia	एशिया (f)	eshiya
Africa	अफ्रीका (m)	afrīka
Australia	ऑस्ट्रेलिया (m)	ostreliya
America	अमेरिका (f)	amerika
North America	उत्तरी अमेरिका (f)	uttarī amerika

South America	दक्षिणी अमेरिका (f)	dakshinī amerika
Antarctica	अंटार्कटिक (m)	antārkatik
the Arctic	आर्कटिक (m)	ārkatik

76. Cardinal directions

north	उत्तर (m)	uttar
to the north	उत्तर की ओर	uttar kī or
in the north	उत्तर में	uttar men
northern (adj)	उत्तरी	uttarī

south	दक्षिण (m)	dakshin
to the south	दक्षिण की ओर	dakshin kī or
in the south	दक्षिण में	dakshin men
southern (adj)	दक्षिणी	dakshinī

west	पश्चिम (m)	pashchim
to the west	पश्चिम की ओर	pashchim kī or
in the west	पश्चिम में	pashchim men
western (adj)	पश्चिमी	pashchimī

east	पूर्व (m)	pūrv
to the east	पूर्व की ओर	pūrv kī or
in the east	पूर्व में	pūrv men
eastern (adj)	पूर्वी	pūrvī

77. Sea. Ocean

sea	सागर (m)	sāgar
ocean	महासागर (m)	mahāsāgar
gulf (bay)	खाड़ी (f)	khārī
straits	जलग्रीवा (m)	jalagrīva

continent (mainland)	महाद्वीप (m)	mahādvīp
island	द्वीप (m)	dvīp
peninsula	प्रायद्वीप (m)	prāyadvīp
archipelago	द्वीप समूह (m)	dvīp samūh

bay, cove	तट-खाड़ी (f)	tat-khārī
harbor	बंदरगाह (m)	bandaragāh
lagoon	लैगून (m)	laigūn
cape	अंतरीप (m)	antarīp

atoll	एटोल (m)	etol
reef	रीफ़ (m)	rīf
coral	प्रवाल (m)	pravāl
coral reef	प्रवाल रीफ़ (m)	pravāl rīf
deep (adj)	गहरा	gahara

depth (deep water)	गहराई (f)	gaharaī
abyss	रसातल (m)	rasātal
trench (e.g., Mariana ~)	गढ़ा (m)	garha

current (Ocean ~)	धारा (f)	dhāra
to surround (bathe)	घिरा होना	ghira hona

shore	किनारा (m)	kināra
coast	तटबंध (m)	tatabandh

flow (flood tide)	ज्वार (m)	jvār
ebb (ebb tide)	भाटा (m)	bhāta
shoal	रेती (m)	retī
bottom (~ of the sea)	तला (m)	tala

wave	तरंग (f)	tarang
crest (~ of a wave)	तरंग शिखर (f)	tarang shikhar
spume (sea foam)	झाग (m)	jhāg

hurricane	तूफ़ान (m)	tufān
tsunami	सुनामी (f)	sunāmī
calm (dead ~)	शांत (m)	shānt
quiet, calm (adj)	शांत	shānt

pole	ध्रुव (m)	dhruv
polar (adj)	ध्रुवीय	dhruvīy

latitude	अक्षांश (m)	akshānsh
longitude	देशान्तर (m)	deshāntar
parallel	समांतर-रेखा (f)	samāntar-rekha
equator	भूमध्य रेखा (f)	bhūmadhy rekha

sky	आकाश (f)	ākāsh
horizon	क्षितिज (m)	kshitij
air	हवा (f)	hava

lighthouse	प्रकाशस्तंभ (m)	prakāshastambh
to dive (vi)	गोता मारना	gota mārana
to sink (ab. boat)	डूब जाना	dūb jāna
treasures	खज़ाना (m)	khazāna

78. Seas' and Oceans' names

Atlantic Ocean	अटलांटिक महासागर (m)	atalāntik mahāsāgar
Indian Ocean	हिन्द महासागर (m)	hind mahāsāgar
Pacific Ocean	प्रशांत महासागर (m)	prashānt mahāsāgar
Arctic Ocean	उत्तरी ध्रुव महासागर (m)	uttarī dhuv mahāsāgar

Black Sea	काला सागर (m)	kāla sāgar
Red Sea	लाल सागर (m)	lāl sāgar

Yellow Sea	पीला सागर (m)	pīla sāgar
White Sea	सफ़ेद सागर (m)	safed sāgar
Caspian Sea	कैस्पियन सागर (m)	kaispiyan sāgar
Dead Sea	मृत सागर (m)	mrt sāgar
Mediterranean Sea	भूमध्य सागर (m)	bhūmadhy sāgar
Aegean Sea	ईजियन सागर (m)	ījiyan sāgar
Adriatic Sea	एड्रिएटिक सागर (m)	edrietik sāgar
Arabian Sea	अरब सागर (m)	arab sāgar
Sea of Japan	जापान सागर (m)	jāpān sāgar
Bering Sea	बेरिंग सागर (m)	bering sāgar
South China Sea	दक्षिण चीन सागर (m)	dakshin chīn sāgar
Coral Sea	कोरल सागर (m)	koral sāgar
Tasman Sea	तस्मान सागर (m)	tasmān sāgar
Caribbean Sea	करिबियन सागर (m)	karibiyan sāgar
Barents Sea	बैरेंट्स सागर (m)	bairents sāgar
Kara Sea	काड़ा सागर (m)	kāra sāgar
North Sea	उतर सागर (m)	uttar sāgar
Baltic Sea	बाल्टिक सागर (m)	bāltik sāgar
Norwegian Sea	नार्वे सागर (m)	nārve sāgar

79. Mountains

mountain	पहाड़ (m)	pahār
mountain range	पर्वत माला (f)	parvat māla
mountain ridge	पहाड़ों का सिलसिला (m)	pahāron ka silasila
summit, top	चोटी (f)	chotī
peak	शिखर (m)	shikhar
foot (~ of the mountain)	तलहटी (f)	talahatī
slope (mountainside)	ढलान (f)	dhalān
volcano	ज्वालामुखी (m)	jvālāmukhī
active volcano	सक्रिय ज्वालामुखी (m)	sakriy jvālāmukhī
dormant volcano	निष्क्रिय ज्वालामुखी (m)	nishkriy jvālāmukhī
eruption	विस्फोटन (m)	visfotan
crater	ज्वालामुखी का मुख (m)	jvālāmukhī ka mukh
magma	मैग्मा (m)	maigma
lava	लावा (m)	lāva
molten (~ lava)	पिघला हुआ	pighala hua
canyon	घाटी (m)	ghātī
gorge	तंग घाटी (f)	tang ghātī
crevice	दरार (m)	darār

pass, col	मार्ग (m)	mārg
plateau	पठार (m)	pathār
cliff	शिला (f)	shila
hill	टीला (m)	tīla

glacier	हिमनद (m)	himanad
waterfall	झरना (m)	jharana
geyser	उष्ण जल स्रोत (m)	ushn jal srot
lake	तालाब (m)	tālāb

plain	समतल प्रदेश (m)	samatal pradesh
landscape	परिदृश्य (m)	paridrshy
echo	गूँज (f)	gūnj

alpinist	पर्वतारोही (m)	parvatārohī
rock climber	पर्वतारोही (m)	parvatārohī
to conquer (in climbing)	चोटी पर पहुँचना	chotī par pahunchana
climb (an easy ~)	चढ़ाव (m)	charhāv

80. Mountains names

The Alps	आल्पस (m)	ālpas
Mont Blanc	मोन्ट ब्लैंक (m)	mont blaink
The Pyrenees	पाइरीनीज़ (f pl)	pairīnīz

The Carpathians	कार्पाथियेन्स (m)	kārpāthiyens
The Ural Mountains	यूराल (m)	yūral
The Caucasus Mountains	कोकेशिया के पहाड़ (m)	kokeshiya ke pahār
Mount Elbrus	एल्ब्रस पर्वत (m)	elbras parvat

The Altai Mountains	अल्टाई पर्वत (m)	altaī parvat
The Tian Shan	तियान शान (m)	tiyān shān
The Pamir Mountains	पामीर पर्वत (m)	pāmīr parvat
The Himalayas	हिमालय (m)	himālay
Mount Everest	माउंट एवरेस्ट (m)	maunt evarest

| The Andes | एंडीज़ (f pl) | endīz |
| Mount Kilimanjaro | किलीमन्जारो (m) | kilīmanjāro |

81. Rivers

river	नदी (f)	nadī
spring (natural source)	झरना (m)	jharana
riverbed (river channel)	नदी तल (m)	nadī tal
basin (river valley)	बेसिन (m)	besin
to flow into …	गिरना	girana
tributary	उपनदी (f)	upanadī
bank (of river)	तट (m)	tat

current (stream)	धारा (f)	dhāra
downstream (adv)	बहाव के साथ	bahāv ke sāth
upstream (adv)	बहाव के विरुद्ध	bahāv ke virūddh
inundation	बाढ़ (f)	bārh
flooding	बाढ़ (f)	bārh
to overflow (vi)	उमड़ना	umarana
to flood (vt)	पानी से भरना	pānī se bharana
shallow (shoal)	छिछला पानी (m)	chhichhala pānī
rapids	तेज़ उतार (m)	tez utār
dam	बांध (m)	bāndh
canal	नहर (f)	nahar
reservoir (artificial lake)	जलाशय (m)	jalāshay
sluice, lock	स्लूस (m)	slūs
water body (pond, etc.)	जल स्रोत (m)	jal srot
swamp (marshland)	दलदल (f)	daladal
bog, marsh	दलदल (f)	daladal
whirlpool	भंवर (m)	bhanvar
stream (brook)	झरना (m)	jharana
drinking (ab. water)	पीने का	pīne ka
fresh (~ water)	ताज़ा	tāza
ice	बर्फ़ (m)	barf
to freeze over (ab. river, etc.)	जम जाना	jam jāna

82. Rivers' names

Seine	सीन (f)	sīn
Loire	लॉयर (f)	loyar
Thames	थेम्स (f)	thems
Rhine	राइन (f)	rain
Danube	डेन्यूब (f)	denyūb
Volga	वोल्गा (f)	volga
Don	डॉन (f)	don
Lena	लेना (f)	lena
Yellow River	ह्वांग हे (f)	hvāng he
Yangtze	यांग्त्ज़ी (f)	yāngtzī
Mekong	मेकांग (f)	mekāng
Ganges	गंगा (f)	ganga
Nile River	नील (f)	nīl
Congo River	कांगो (f)	kāngo

Okavango River	ओकावान्गो (f)	okāvāngo
Zambezi River	ज़म्बेज़ी (f)	zambezī
Limpopo River	लिम्पोपो (f)	limpopo
Mississippi River	मिसिसिपी (f)	misisipī

83. Forest

forest, wood	जंगल (m)	jangal
forest (as adj)	जंगली	jangalī
thick forest	घना जंगल (m)	ghana jangal
grove	उपवान (m)	upavān
forest clearing	खुला छोटा मैदान (m)	khula chhota maidān
thicket	झाड़ियाँ (f pl)	jhāriyān
scrubland	झाड़ियों भरा मैदान (m)	jhāriyon bhara maidān
footpath (troddenpath)	फुटपाथ (m)	futapāth
gully	नाली (f)	nālī
tree	पेड़ (m)	per
leaf	पत्ता (m)	patta
leaves (foliage)	पत्तियां (f)	pattiyān
fall of leaves	पतझड़ (m)	patajhar
to fall (ab. leaves)	गिरना	girana
top (of the tree)	शिखर (m)	shikhar
branch	टहनी (f)	tahanī
bough	शाखा (f)	shākha
bud (on shrub, tree)	कलिका (f)	kalika
needle (of pine tree)	सुई (f)	suī
pine cone	शंकुफल (m)	shankufal
hollow (in a tree)	खोखला (m)	khokhala
nest	घोंसला (m)	ghonsala
burrow (animal hole)	बिल (m)	bil
trunk	तना (m)	tana
root	जड़ (f)	jar
bark	छाल (f)	chhāl
moss	काई (f)	kaī
to uproot (remove trees or tree stumps)	उखाड़ना	ukhārana
to chop down	काटना	kātana
to deforest (vt)	जंगल काटना	jangal kātana
tree stump	ठूंठ (m)	thūnth
campfire	अलाव (m)	alāv
forest fire	जंगल की आग (f)	jangal kī āg

to extinguish (vt)	आग बुझाना	āg bujhāna
forest ranger	वनरक्षक (m)	vanarakshak
protection	रक्षा (f)	raksha
to protect (~ nature)	रक्षा करना	raksha karana
poacher	चोर शिकारी (m)	chor shikārī
steel trap	फंदा (m)	fanda

| to gather, to pick (vt) | बटोरना | batorana |
| to lose one's way | रास्ता भूलना | rāsta bhūlana |

84. Natural resources

natural resources	प्राकृतिक संसाधन (m pl)	prākrtik sansādhan
minerals	खनिज पदार्थ (m pl)	khanij padārth
deposits	तह (f pl)	tah
field (e.g., oilfield)	क्षेत्र (m)	kshetr

to mine (extract)	खोदना	khodana
mining (extraction)	खनिकर्म (m)	khanikarm
ore	अयस्क (m)	ayask
mine (e.g., for coal)	खान (f)	khān
shaft (mine ~)	शैफ़ट (m)	shaifat
miner	खनिक (m)	khanik

| gas (natural ~) | गैस (m) | gais |
| gas pipeline | गैस पाइप लाइन (m) | gais paip lain |

oil (petroleum)	पेट्रोल (m)	petrol
oil pipeline	तेल पाइप लाइन (m)	tel paip lain
oil well	तेल का कुँआ (m)	tel ka kuna
derrick (tower)	डेरिक (m)	derik
tanker	टैंकर (m)	tainkar

sand	रेत (m)	ret
limestone	चूना पत्थर (m)	chūna patthar
gravel	बजरी (f)	bajarī
peat	पीट (m)	pīt
clay	मिट्टी (f)	mittī
coal	कोयला (m)	koyala

iron (ore)	लोहा (m)	loha
gold	सोना (m)	sona
silver	चाँदी (f)	chāndī
nickel	गिलट (m)	gilat
copper	ताँबा (m)	tānba

zinc	जस्ता (m)	jasta
manganese	अयस (m)	ayas
mercury	पारा (f)	pāra
lead	सीसा (f)	sīsa

mineral	खनिज (m)	khanij
crystal	क्रिस्टल (m)	kristal
marble	संगमरमर (m)	sangamaramar
uranium	यूरेनियम (m)	yūreniyam

85. Weather

weather	मौसम (m)	mausam
weather forecast	मौसम का पूर्वानुमान (m)	mausam ka pūrvānumān
temperature	तापमान (m)	tāpamān
thermometer	थर्मामीटर (m)	tharmāmītar
barometer	बैरोमीटर (m)	bairomītar
humidity	नमी (f)	namī
heat (extreme ~)	गरमी (f)	garamī
hot (torrid)	गरम	garam
it's hot	गरमी है	garamī hai
it's warm	गरम है	garam hai
warm (moderately hot)	गरम	garam
it's cold	ठंडक है	thandak hai
cold (adj)	ठंडा	thanda
sun	सूरज (m)	sūraj
to shine (vi)	चमकना	chamakana
sunny (day)	धूपदार	dhūpadār
to come up (vi)	उगना	ugana
to set (vi)	डूबना	dūbana
cloud	बादल (m)	bādal
cloudy (adj)	मेघाच्छादित	meghāchchhādit
rain cloud	घना बादल (m)	ghana bādal
somber (gloomy)	बदली	badalī
rain	बारिश (f)	bārish
it's raining	बारिश हो रही है	bārish ho rahī hai
rainy (~ day, weather)	बरसाती	barasātī
to drizzle (vi)	बूंदाबांदी होना	būndābāndī hona
pouring rain	मूसलधार बारिश (f)	mūsaladhār bārish
downpour	मूसलधार बारिश (f)	mūsaladhār bārish
heavy (e.g., ~ rain)	भारी	bhārī
puddle	पोखर (m)	pokhar
to get wet (in rain)	भीगना	bhīgana
fog (mist)	कुहरा (m)	kuhara
foggy	कुहरेदार	kuharedār
snow	बर्फ़ (f)	barf
it's snowing	बर्फ़ पड़ रही है	barf par rahī hai

86. Severe weather. Natural disasters

thunderstorm	गरजवाला तुफान (m)	garajavāla tufān
lightning (~ strike)	बिजली (m)	bijalī
to flash (vi)	चमकना	chamakana
thunder	गरज (m)	garaj
to thunder (vi)	बादल गरजना	bādal garajana
it's thundering	बादल गरज रहा है	bādal garaj raha hai
hail	ओला (m)	ola
it's hailing	ओले पड़ रहे हैं	ole par rahe hain
to flood (vt)	बाढ़ आ जाना	bārh ā jāna
flood, inundation	बाढ़ (f)	bārh
earthquake	भूकंप (m)	bhūkamp
tremor, quake	झटका (m)	jhataka
epicenter	अधिकेंद्र (m)	adhikendr
eruption	उद्गार (m)	udgār
lava	लावा (m)	lāva
twister	बवंडर (m)	bavandar
tornado	टोर्नेडो (m)	tornedo
typhoon	रतूफान (m)	ratūfān
hurricane	समुद्री तूफान (m)	samudrī tūfān
storm	तुफ़ान (m)	tufān
tsunami	सुनामी (f)	sunāmī
cyclone	चक्रवात (m)	chakravāt
bad weather	ख़राब मौसम (m)	kharāb mausam
fire (accident)	आग (f)	āg
disaster	प्रलय (m)	pralay
meteorite	उल्का पिंड (m)	ulka pind
avalanche	हिमस्खलन (m)	himaskhalan
snowslide	हिमस्खलन (m)	himaskhalan
blizzard	बर्फ़ का तूफान (m)	barf ka tufān
snowstorm	बर्फ़ीला तूफान (m)	barfila tufān

FAUNA

87. Mammals. Predators

predator	परभक्षी (m)	parabhakshī
tiger	बाघ (m)	bāgh
lion	शेर (m)	sher
wolf	भेड़िया (m)	bheriya
fox	लोमड़ी (f)	lomri
jaguar	जागुआर (m)	jāguār
leopard	तेंदुआ (m)	tendua
cheetah	चीता (m)	chīta
black panther	काला तेंदुआ (m)	kāla tendua
puma	पहाड़ी बिलाव (m)	pahādī bilāv
snow leopard	हिम तेंदुआ (m)	him tendua
lynx	वन बिलाव (m)	van bilāv
coyote	कोयोट (m)	koyot
jackal	गीदड़ (m)	gīdar
hyena	लकड़बग्घा (m)	lakarabaggha

88. Wild animals

animal	जानवर (m)	jānavar
beast (animal)	जानवर (m)	jānavar
squirrel	गिलहरी (f)	gilaharī
hedgehog	कांटा-चूहा (m)	kānta-chūha
hare	खरगोश (m)	kharagosh
rabbit	खरगोश (m)	kharagosh
badger	बिज्जू (m)	bijjū
raccoon	रैकून (m)	raikūn
hamster	हैम्स्टर (m)	haimstar
marmot	मारमोट (m)	māramot
mole	छछूंदर (m)	chhachhūndar
mouse	चूहा (m)	chūha
rat	घूस (m)	ghūs
bat	चमगादड़ (m)	chamagādar
ermine	नेवला (m)	nevala
sable	सेबल (m)	sebal

marten	मारटेन (m)	māraten
weasel	नेवला (m)	nevala
mink	मिंक (m)	mink
beaver	ऊदबिलाव (m)	ūdabilāv
otter	ऊदबिलाव (m)	ūdabilāv
horse	घोड़ा (m)	ghora
moose	मूस (m)	mūs
deer	हिरण (m)	hiran
camel	ऊंट (m)	ūnt
bison	बाइसन (m)	baisan
aurochs	जंगली बैल (m)	jangalī bail
buffalo	भैंस (m)	bhains
zebra	ज़ेबरा (m)	zebara
antelope	मृग (f)	mrg
roe deer	मृग्नी (f)	mrgnī
fallow deer	चीतल (m)	chītal
chamois	शैमी (f)	shaimī
wild boar	जंगली सुअार (m)	jangalī suār
whale	ह्वेल (f)	hvel
seal	सील (m)	sīl
walrus	वॉलरस (m)	volaras
fur seal	फर सील (f)	far sīl
dolphin	डॉल्फ़िन (f)	dolafin
bear	रीछ (m)	rīchh
polar bear	सफ़ेद रीछ (m)	safed rīchh
panda	पांडा (m)	pānda
monkey	बंदर (m)	bandar
chimpanzee	वनमानुष (m)	vanamānush
orangutan	वनमानुष (m)	vanamānush
gorilla	गोरिला (m)	gorila
macaque	अफ़्रिकन लंगूर (m)	afrikan langūr
gibbon	गिब्बन (m)	gibban
elephant	हाथी (m)	hāthī
rhinoceros	गैंडा (m)	gainda
giraffe	जिराफ़ (m)	jirāf
hippopotamus	दरियाई घोड़ा (m)	dariyaī ghora
kangaroo	कंगारू (m)	kangārū
koala (bear)	कोआला (m)	koāla
mongoose	नेवला (m)	nevala
chinchilla	चिनचीला (f)	chinachīla
skunk	स्कंक (m)	skank
porcupine	शल्यक (f)	shalyak

89. Domestic animals

cat	बिल्ली (f)	billī
tomcat	बिल्ला (m)	billa
dog	कुत्ता (m)	kutta
horse	घोड़ा (m)	ghora
stallion (male horse)	घोड़ा (m)	ghora
mare	घोड़ी (f)	ghorī
cow	गाय (f)	gāy
bull	बैल (m)	bail
ox	बैल (m)	bail
sheep (ewe)	भेड़ (f)	bher
ram	भेड़ा (m)	bhera
goat	बकरी (f)	bakarī
billy goat, he-goat	बकरा (m)	bakara
donkey	गधा (m)	gadha
mule	खच्चर (m)	khachchar
pig, hog	सुअर (m)	suar
piglet	घेंटा (m)	ghenta
rabbit	खरगोश (m)	kharagosh
hen (chicken)	मुर्गी (f)	murgī
rooster	मुर्गा (m)	murga
duck	बत्तख़ (f)	battakh
drake	नर बत्तख़ (m)	nar battakh
goose	हंस (m)	hans
tom turkey, gobbler	नर टर्की (m)	nar tarkī
turkey (hen)	टर्की (f)	tarkī
domestic animals	घरेलू पशु (m pl)	gharelū pashu
tame (e.g., ~ hamster)	पालतू	pālatū
to tame (vt)	पालतू बनाना	pālatū banāna
to breed (vt)	पालना	pālana
farm	खेत (m)	khet
poultry	मुर्गी पालन (f)	murgī pālan
cattle	मवेशी (m)	maveshī
herd (cattle)	पशु समूह (m)	pashu samūh
stable	अस्तबल (m)	astabal
pigpen	सूअरखाना (m)	sūarakhāna
cowshed	गोशाला (f)	goshāla
rabbit hutch	खरगोश का दरबा (m)	kharagosh ka daraba
hen house	मुर्गीखाना (m)	murgīkhāna

90. Birds

bird	चिड़िया (f)	chiriya
pigeon	कबूतर (m)	kabūtar
sparrow	गौरैया (f)	gauraiya
tit (great tit)	टिटरी (f)	titarī
magpie	नीलकण्ठ पक्षी (f)	nīlakanth pakshī

raven	काला कौआ (m)	kāla kaua
crow	कौआ (m)	kaua
jackdaw	कौआ (m)	kaua
rook	कौआ (m)	kaua

duck	बत्तख़ (f)	battakh
goose	हंस (m)	hans
pheasant	तीतर (m)	tītar

eagle	चील (f)	chīl
hawk	बाज़ (m)	bāz
falcon	बाज़ (m)	bāz
vulture	गिद्ध (m)	giddh
condor (Andean ~)	कॉन्डोर (m)	kondor

swan	राजहंस (m)	rājahans
crane	सारस (m)	sāras
stork	लकलक (m)	lakalak

parrot	तोता (m)	tota
hummingbird	हमिंग बर्ड (f)	haming bard
peacock	मोर (m)	mor

ostrich	शुतुरमुर्ग (m)	shuturamurg
heron	बगुला (m)	bagula
flamingo	फ़्लेमिन्गो (m)	flemingo
pelican	हवासिल (m)	havāsil

| nightingale | बुलबुल (m) | bulabul |
| swallow | अबाबील (f) | abābīl |

thrush	मुखव्रण (f)	mukhavran
song thrush	मुखव्रण (f)	mukhavran
blackbird	ब्लैकबर्ड (m)	blaikabard

swift	बतासी (f)	batāsī
lark	भरत (m)	bharat
quail	वर्तक (m)	varttak

woodpecker	कठफोड़ा (m)	kathafora
cuckoo	कोयल (f)	koyal
owl	उल्लू (m)	ullū
eagle owl	गरुड़ उल्लू (m)	garūr ullū

wood grouse	तीतर (m)	tītar
black grouse	काला तीतर (m)	kāla tītar
partridge	चकोर (m)	chakor
starling	तिलिया (f)	tiliya
canary	कनारी (f)	kanārī
hazel grouse	पिंगल तीतर (m)	pingal tītar
chaffinch	फ़िंच (m)	finch
bullfinch	बुलफ़िंच (m)	bulafinch
seagull	गंगा-चिल्ली (f)	ganga-chillī
albatross	अल्बात्रोस (m)	albātros
penguin	पेंगुइन (m)	penguin

91. Fish. Marine animals

bream	ब्रीम (f)	brīm
carp	कार्प (f)	kārp
perch	पर्च (f)	parch
catfish	कैटफ़िश (f)	kaitafish
pike	पाइक (f)	paik
salmon	सैल्मन (f)	sailman
sturgeon	स्टर्जन (f)	starjan
herring	हेरिंग (f)	hering
Atlantic salmon	अटलांटिक सैल्मन (f)	atalāntik sailman
mackerel	माक्रैल (f)	mākrail
flatfish	फ़्लैटफ़िश (f)	flaitafish
zander, pike perch	पाइक पर्च (f)	paik parch
cod	कॉड (f)	kod
tuna	टूना (f)	tūna
trout	ट्राउट (f)	traut
eel	सर्पमीन (f)	sarpamīn
electric ray	विद्युत शंकुश (f)	vidyut shankush
moray eel	मोरे सर्पमीन (f)	more sarpamīn
piranha	पिरान्हा (f)	pirānha
shark	शार्क (f)	shārk
dolphin	डॉल्फ़िन (f)	dolafin
whale	ह्वेल (f)	hvel
crab	केकड़ा (m)	kekara
jellyfish	जेली फ़िश (f)	jelī fish
octopus	आक्टोपस (m)	āktopas
starfish	स्टार फ़िश (f)	stār fish
sea urchin	जलसाही (f)	jalasāhī

seahorse	समुद्री घोड़ा (m)	samudrī ghora
oyster	कस्तूरा (m)	kastūra
shrimp	झींगा (f)	jhīnga
lobster	लॉब्सटर (m)	lobsatar
spiny lobster	स्पाइनी लॉब्सटर (m)	spainī lobsatar

92. Amphibians. Reptiles

| snake | सर्प (m) | sarp |
| venomous (snake) | विषैला | vishaila |

viper	वाइपर (m)	vaipar
cobra	नाग (m)	nāg
python	अजगर (m)	ajagar
boa	अजगर (m)	ajagar

grass snake	साँप (f)	sānp
rattle snake	रैटल सर्प (m)	raital sarp
anaconda	एनाकोन्डा (f)	enākonda

lizard	छिपकली (f)	chhipakalī
iguana	इग्युएना (m)	igyūena
monitor lizard	मॉनिटर छिपकली (f)	monitar chhipakalī
salamander	सैलामैंडर (m)	sailāmaindar
chameleon	गिरगिट (m)	giragit
scorpion	वृश्चिक (m)	vrshchik

turtle	कछुआ (m)	kachhua
frog	मेंढक (m)	mendhak
toad	भेक (m)	bhek
crocodile	मगर (m)	magar

93. Insects

insect, bug	कीट (m)	kīt
butterfly	तितली (f)	titalī
ant	चींटी (f)	chīntī
fly	मक्खी (f)	makkhī
mosquito	मच्छर (m)	machchhar
beetle	भृंग (m)	bhrng

wasp	हड्डा (m)	hadda
bee	मधुमक्खी (f)	madhumakkhī
bumblebee	भंवरा (m)	bhanvara
gadfly (botfly)	गोमक्खी (f)	gomakkhī

| spider | मकड़ी (f) | makarī |
| spiderweb | मकड़ी का जाल (m) | makarī ka jāl |

dragonfly	व्याध-पतंग (m)	vyādh-patang
grasshopper	टिड्डा (m)	tidda
moth (night butterfly)	पतंगा (m)	patanga

cockroach	तिलचट्टा (m)	tilachatta
tick	जुँआ (m)	juna
flea	पिस्सू (m)	pissū
midge	भुनगा (m)	bhunaga

locust	टिड्डी (f)	tiddī
snail	घोंघा (m)	ghongha
cricket	झींगुर (m)	jhīngur
lightning bug	जुगनू (m)	juganū
ladybug	सोनपंखी (f)	sonapankhī
cockchafer	कोकचाफ़ (m)	kokachāf

leech	जोक (m)	jok
caterpillar	इल्ली (f)	illī
earthworm	कंचुआ (m)	kenchua
larva	कीटडिंभ (m)	kītadimbh

FLORA

94. Trees

tree	पेड़ (m)	per
deciduous (adj)	पर्णपाती	parnapātī
coniferous (adj)	शंकुधर	shankudhar
evergreen (adj)	सदाबहार	sadābahār
apple tree	सेब वृक्ष (m)	seb vrksh
pear tree	नाशपाती का पेड़ (m)	nāshpātī ka per
cherry tree	चेरी का पेड़ (f)	cherī ka per
plum tree	आलूबुख़ारे का पेड़ (m)	ālūbukhāre ka per
birch	सनोबर का पेड़ (m)	sanobar ka per
oak	बलूत (m)	balūt
linden tree	लिनडेन वृक्ष (m)	linaden vrksh
aspen	आस्पेन वृक्ष (m)	āspen vrksh
maple	मेपल (m)	mepal
spruce	फर का पेड़ (m)	far ka per
pine	देवदार (m)	devadār
larch	लार्च (m)	lārch
fir tree	फर (m)	far
cedar	देवदर (m)	devadar
poplar	पोप्लर वृक्ष (m)	poplar vrksh
rowan	रोवाण (m)	rovān
willow	विलो (f)	vilo
alder	आल्डर वृक्ष (m)	āldar vrksh
beech	बीच (m)	bīch
elm	एल्म वृक्ष (m)	elm vrksh
ash (tree)	एश-वृक्ष (m)	esh-vrksh
chestnut	चेस्टनट (m)	chestanat
magnolia	मैगनोलिया (f)	maiganoliya
palm tree	ताड़ का पेड़ (m)	tār ka per
cypress	सरो (m)	saro
mangrove	मैनग्रोव (m)	mainagrov
baobab	गोरक्षी (m)	gorakshī
eucalyptus	यूकेलिप्टस (m)	yūkeliptas
sequoia	सकोइया (f)	sekoiya

95. Shrubs

bush	झाड़ी (f)	jhārī
shrub	झाड़ी (f)	jhārī

grapevine	अंगूर की बेल (f)	angūr kī bel
vineyard	अंगूर का बाग़ (m)	angūr ka bāg

raspberry bush	रास्पबेरी की झाड़ी (f)	rāspaberī kī jhārī
redcurrant bush	लाल करेंट की झाड़ी (f)	lāl karent kī jhārī
gooseberry bush	गूज़बेरी की झाड़ी (f)	gūzaberī kī jhārī

acacia	ऐकेशिय (m)	aikeshiy
barberry	बारबेरी झाड़ी (f)	bāraberī jhārī
jasmine	चमेली (f)	chamelī

juniper	जूनिपर (m)	jūnipar
rosebush	गुलाब की झाड़ी (f)	gulāb kī jhārī
dog rose	जंगली गुलाब (m)	jangalī gulāb

96. Fruits. Berries

fruit	फल (m)	fal
fruits	फल (m pl)	fal
apple	सेब (m)	seb
pear	नाश्पाती (f)	nāshpātī
plum	आलूबुख़ारा (m)	ālūbukhāra

strawberry (garden ~)	स्ट्रॉबेरी (f)	stroberī
cherry	चेरी (f)	cherī
grape	अंगूर (m)	angūr

raspberry	रास्पबेरी (f)	rāspaberī
blackcurrant	काली करेंट (f)	kālī karent
redcurrant	लाल करेंट (f)	lāl karent
gooseberry	गूज़बेरी (f)	gūzaberī
cranberry	क्रेनबेरी (f)	krenaberī

orange	संतरा (m)	santara
mandarin	नारंगी (f)	nārangī
pineapple	अनानास (m)	anānās
banana	केला (m)	kela
date	खजूर (m)	khajūr

lemon	नींबू (m)	nīmbū
apricot	ख़ूबानी (f)	khūbānī
peach	आड़ू (m)	ārū
kiwi	चीकू (m)	chīkū
grapefruit	ग्रेपफ्रूट (m)	grepafrūt

berry	बेरी (f)	berī
berries	बेरियां (f pl)	beriyān
cowberry	काओबेरी (f)	kaoberī
wild strawberry	जंगली स्ट्रॉबेरी (f)	jangalī stroberī
bilberry	बिलबेरी (f)	bilaberī

97. Flowers. Plants

| flower | फूल (m) | fūl |
| bouquet (of flowers) | गुलदस्ता (m) | guladasta |

rose (flower)	गुलाब (f)	gulāb
tulip	ट्यूलिप (m)	tyūlip
carnation	गुलनार (m)	gulanār
gladiolus	ग्लेडियोलस (m)	glediyolas

cornflower	नीलकूपी (m)	nīlakūpī
harebell	ब्लूबेल (m)	blūbel
dandelion	कुकरौंधा (m)	kukaraundha
camomile	कैमोमाइल (m)	kaimomail

aloe	मुसब्बर (m)	musabbar
cactus	कैक्टस (m)	kaiktas
rubber plant, ficus	रबड़ का पौधा (m)	rabar ka paudha

lily	कुमुदिनी (f)	kumudinī
geranium	जेरेनियम (m)	jeraniyam
hyacinth	हायसिंथ (m)	hāyasinth

mimosa	मिमोसा (m)	mimosa
narcissus	नरगीस (f)	naragis
nasturtium	नस्टाशयम (m)	nastāshayam

orchid	आर्किड (m)	ārkid
peony	पियोनी (m)	piyonī
violet	वॉयलेट (m)	voyalet

pansy	पैंज़ी (m pl)	painzī
forget-me-not	फर्गेट मी नाट (m)	fargent mī nāt
daisy	गुलबहार (f)	gulabahār

poppy	खशखाश (m)	khashakhāsh
hemp	भांग (f)	bhāng
mint	पुदीना (m)	pudīna

| lily of the valley | कामुदिनी (f) | kāmudinī |
| snowdrop | सफ़ेद फूल (m) | safed fūl |

| nettle | बिच्छू बूटी (f) | bichchhū būtī |
| sorrel | सोरेल (m) | sorel |

water lily	कुमुदिनी (f)	kumudinī
fern	फर्न (m)	farn
lichen	शैवाक (m)	shaivāk
greenhouse (tropical ~)	शीशाघर (m)	shīshāghar
lawn	घास का मैदान (m)	ghās ka maidān
flowerbed	फुलवारी (f)	fulavārī
plant	पौधा (m)	paudha
grass	घास (f)	ghās
blade of grass	तिनका (m)	tinaka
leaf	पत्ती (f)	pattī
petal	पंखड़ी (f)	pankharī
stem	डंडी (f)	dandī
tuber	कंद (m)	kand
young plant (shoot)	अंकुर (m)	ankur
thorn	कांटा (m)	kānta
to blossom (vi)	खिलना	khilana
to fade, to wither	मुरझाना	murajhāna
smell (odor)	बू (m)	bū
to cut (flowers)	काटना	kātana
to pick (a flower)	तोड़ना	torana

98. Cereals, grains

grain	दाना (m)	dāna
cereal crops	अनाज की फ़सलें (m pl)	anāj kī fasalen
ear (of barley, etc.)	बाल (f)	bāl
wheat	गेहूं (m)	gehūn
rye	रई (f)	raī
oats	जई (f)	jaī
millet	बाजरा (m)	bājara
barley	जौ (m)	jau
corn	मक्का (m)	makka
rice	चावल (m)	chāval
buckwheat	मोथी (m)	mothī
pea plant	मटर (m)	matar
kidney bean	राजमा (f)	rājama
soy	सोया (m)	soya
lentil	दाल (m)	dāl
beans (pulse crops)	फली (f pl)	falī

COUNTRIES OF THE WORLD

99. Countries. Part 1

Afghanistan	अफ़ग़ानिस्तान (m)	afagānistān
Albania	अल्बानिया (m)	albāniya
Argentina	अर्जेंटीना (m)	arjentīna
Armenia	आर्मीनिया (m)	ārmīniya
Australia	आस्ट्रेलिया (m)	āstreliya
Austria	ऑसट्रिया (m)	ostriya
Azerbaijan	आज़रबाइजान (m)	āzarabaijān
The Bahamas	बहामा (m)	bahāma
Bangladesh	बांग्लादेश (m)	bānglādesh
Belarus	बेलारूस (m)	belārūs
Belgium	बेल्जियम (m)	beljiyam
Bolivia	बोलीविया (m)	bolīviya
Bosnia and Herzegovina	बोस्निया और हर्ज़ेगोविना	bosniya aur harzegovina
Brazil	ब्राज़ील (m)	brāzīl
Bulgaria	बुल्गारिया (m)	bulgāriya
Cambodia	कम्बोडिया (m)	kambodiya
Canada	कनाडा (m)	kanāda
Chile	चिली (m)	chilī
China	चीन (m)	chīn
Colombia	कोलम्बिया (m)	kolambiya
Croatia	क्रोएशिया (m)	kroeshiya
Cuba	क्यूबा (m)	kyūba
Cyprus	साइप्रस (m)	saipras
Czech Republic	चेक गणतंत्र (m)	chek ganatantr
Denmark	डेन्मार्क (m)	denmārk
Dominican Republic	डोमिनिकन रिपब्लिक (m)	dominikan ripablik
Ecuador	इक्वेडोर (m)	ikvedor
Egypt	मिस्र (m)	misr
England	इंग्लैंड (m)	inglaind
Estonia	एस्तोनिया (m)	estoniya
Finland	फ़िनलैंड (m)	finalaind
France	फ़्रांस (m)	frāns
French Polynesia	फ्रेंच पॉलीनेशिया (m)	french polīneshiya
Georgia	जॉर्जिया (m)	jorjiya
Germany	जर्मन (m)	jarman
Ghana	घाना (m)	ghāna
Great Britain	ग्रेट ब्रिटेन (m)	gret briten
Greece	ग्रीस (m)	grīs

| Haiti | हाइटी (m) | haitī |
| Hungary | हंगरी (m) | hangarī |

100. Countries. Part 2

Iceland	आयसलैंड (m)	āyasalaind
India	भारत (m)	bhārat
Indonesia	इण्डोनेशिया (m)	indoneshiya
Iran	इरान (m)	irān
Iraq	इराक़ (m)	irāq
Ireland	आयरलैंड (m)	āyaralaind
Israel	इसायल (m)	isrāyal
Italy	इटली (m)	italī

Jamaica	जमैका (m)	jamaika
Japan	जापान (m)	jāpān
Jordan	जॉर्डन (m)	jordan
Kazakhstan	कज़ाकस्तान (m)	kazākastān
Kenya	केन्या (m)	kenya
Kirghizia	किर्गीज़िया (m)	kirgīziya
Kuwait	कुवैत (m)	kuvait

Laos	लाओस (m)	laos
Latvia	लाटविया (m)	lātaviya
Lebanon	लेबनान (m)	lebanān
Libya	लीबिया (m)	lībiya
Liechtenstein	लिकटेंस्टीन (m)	likatenstīn
Lithuania	लिथुआनिया (m)	lithuāniya
Luxembourg	लक्ज़मबर्ग (m)	lakzamabarg

Macedonia (Republic of ~)	मेसेडोनिया (m)	mesedoniya
Madagascar	मडागास्कार (m)	madāgāskār
Malaysia	मलेशिया (m)	maleshiya
Malta	माल्टा (m)	mālta
Mexico	मेक्सिको (m)	meksiko
Moldova, Moldavia	मोलदोवा (m)	moladova

Monaco	मोनाको (m)	monāko
Mongolia	मंगोलिया (m)	mangoliya
Montenegro	मोंटेनेग्रो (m)	montenegro

| Morocco | मोरक्को (m) | morakko |
| Myanmar | म्यांमर (m) | myāmmar |

Namibia	नामीबिया (m)	nāmībiya
Nepal	नेपाल (m)	nepāl
Netherlands	नीदरलैंड्स (m)	nīdaralainds
New Zealand	न्यू ज़ीलैंड (m)	nyū zīlaind
North Korea	उत्तर कोरिया (m)	uttar koriya
Norway	नार्वे (m)	nārve

101. Countries. Part 3

Pakistan	पाकिस्तान (m)	pākistān
Palestine	फिलिस्तीन (m)	filistīn
Panama	पनामा (m)	panāma
Paraguay	परागुआ (m)	parāgua
Peru	पेरू (m)	perū
Poland	पोलैंड (m)	polaind
Portugal	पुर्तगाल (m)	purtagāl
Romania	रोमानिया (m)	romāniya
Russia	रूस (m)	rūs
Saudi Arabia	सऊदी अरब (m)	saūdī arab
Scotland	स्कॉटलैंड (m)	skotalaind
Senegal	सेनेगाल (m)	senegāl
Serbia	सर्बिया (m)	sarbiya
Slovakia	स्लोवाकिया (m)	slovākiya
Slovenia	स्लोवेनिया (m)	sloveniya
South Africa	दक्षिण अफ़्रीका (m)	dakshin afrīka
South Korea	दक्षिण कोरिया (m)	dakshin koriya
Spain	स्पेन (m)	spen
Suriname	सूरीनाम (m)	sūrīnām
Sweden	स्वीडन (m)	svīdan
Switzerland	स्विट्ज़रलैंड (m)	svitzaralaind
Syria	सीरिया (m)	sīriya
Taiwan	ताइवान (m)	taivān
Tajikistan	ताजिकिस्तान (m)	tājikistān
Tanzania	तंज़ानिया (m)	tanzāniya
Tasmania	तास्मानिया (m)	tāsmāniya
Thailand	थाईलैंड (m)	thaīlaind
Tunisia	ट्यूनीसिया (m)	tyunīsiya
Turkey	तुर्की (m)	turkī
Turkmenistan	तुर्कमानिस्तान (m)	turkamānistān
Ukraine	यूक्रेन (m)	yūkren
United Arab Emirates	संयुक्त अरब अमीरात (m)	sanyukt arab amīrāt
United States of America	संयुक्त राज्य अमरीका (m)	sanyukt rājy amarīka
Uruguay	उरुग्वे (m)	urugve
Uzbekistan	उज़्बेकिस्तान (m)	uzbekistān
Vatican	वेटिकन (m)	vetikan
Venezuela	वेनेज़ुएला (m)	venezuela
Vietnam	वियतनाम (m)	viyatanām
Zanzibar	ज़ैंज़िबार (m)	zainzibār

www.ingramcontent.com/pod-product-compliance
Lightning Source LLC
Chambersburg PA
CBHW070815050426
42452CB00011B/2061